# Through the Valley of the Shadow

## A Guide for the Care of the Dying and Their Loved Ones

By
Louis Richard Batzler

Hidden Valley Press
7051 Poole Jones Road
P.O. Box 606
Frederick, Maryland 21701

# THROUGH THE VALLEY OF THE SHADOW
## A Guide for the Care of the Dying and Their Loved Ones

Copyright 1983 Louis Richard Batzler

Please direct all inquiries to:
 Hidden Valley Press
 7051 Poole Jones Road
 P.O. Box 606
 Frederick, Maryland 21701

Cover and text photos by George and Margaret Khoury

First Printing, 1983

Printed in U.S.A.

Library of Congress Catalog Number: 83–11282

ISBN: 0-935710-05-1

# DEDICATION

To Evelyn, my wife, and our
children, Margaret, Louis and Lloyd,
who have journeyed with me in the light
and the shadows.

# ACKNOWLEDGEMENTS

Life is formed through relationships. Thus, in the larger sense, every person who has touched my life has had a part in this book. Persons of all ages from every walk of life, those living and those now dead, have their imprint on the pages that follow. Many of these are nurses who have shared their experiences in the Death and Dying seminars which I have conducted for the *Gotach Center for Health* during the last two years. To all of these unnamed persons, I am most thankful.

I am grateful also to the many writers and researchers whose works I have consulted. Their insights and perspectives are exceedingly valuable. All of these have enriched lives through their contributions toward the understanding of and coping with death.

I especially appreciate the encouragement of my colleague, Nicola M. Tauraso, Director of the *Gotach Center for Health*, and his support of my writing and publishing of this book.

Finally, I am grateful to Debra Palmer and Ruth Brown for typing the manuscript.

For permission to use brief extracts from copyright material, I express my appreciation to the following publishers and authors.

A Kempis, T. *The Imitation of Christ*. London and Basingstocke: MacMillan & Co., 1910, 53–57.

Bean, W. B. "On Death." *Archives of Internal Medicine*, V. 101, June, 1958, 201. Copyright 1958–63, American Medical Association.

Chardin, P.T. *On Suffering* (1974) English translation copyright, 1965, 1960. NY: Harper & Row, Publishers, Inc., 9–10, 32, 83–84.

Feifel, H. *New Meanings of Death*. NY: McGraw-Hill, 1977, 70.

Laforet, E. G. "The Hopeless Case." *Archives of Internal Medicine*, V. 112, September, 1963, 317. Copyright 1958–63, American Medical Association.

Levi. *The Aquarian Gospel of Jesus the Christ*. Marina del Rey, CA: DeVorss & Co., 1972, 95–96.

Silverman, M. (Ed.) *High Holiday Prayer Book*. Bridgeport, CT: Prayer Book Press, 1951, 322.

# CONTENTS

*Nothing is more creative than death, since it is the whole secret of life. It means that the past must be abandoned, that the unknown cannot be avoided, that "I" cannot continue, and that nothing can be ultimately fixed.*

Alan Watts

*Then Almitra spoke, saying, "We would ask now of Death." And he said: "You would know the secret of death. But how shall you find it unless you seek it in the heart of life? The owl whose night-bound eyes are blind unto the day cannot unveil the mystery of light. If you would indeed behold the spirit of death, open your heart wide unto the body of life. For life and death are one, even as the river and sea are one."*

Kahlil Gibran

*Death is the supreme festival on the road to freedom.*

Dietrich Bonhoeffer

*Think not of death as final enemy,*
*Ever seeking to conquer you in strife,*
*But know death is striving to help you see,*
*The meaning of your present precious life.*

Louis Richard Batzler

*The prince who kept the world in awe,*
*The judge whose dictate fix'd the law;*
*The rich, the poor, the great, the small,*
*Are levell'd; death confounds 'em all.*

John Gay

# Preface

Death informs life. Whenever we contemplate the meaning of life, we must inevitably face the reality of death. Death is a great teacher. The universality and the finality of death reveal the potentiality that death has for casting light on life's purposes. The reality of the event of death and the process of dying challenge our values, threaten our identity, modify our goals, restrict our choices, limit our controls, qualify our relationships, disrupt our plans and call into question the meaning of our past, present and future. Death confronts us with our basic nature, our very selfhood, and increases our awareness, sensitivity and growth.

Death is that human experience that reveals our commonality and shows us that the integration and growth of self is related to the integration and growth of the whole human race. For example, when a loved one dies, we experience, to some extent, our own death, and to experience our death in this way is to find new life. The death of a loved one opens new spaces in our consciousness, new ways of remembering, appreciating, loving — of loving not only the deceased, but also of loving humanity, for suffering usually makes us more compassionate. The dying and the dead teach us the meaning of relationships. It might even be said that we do not really know another until he is dead.

Death as an ever-present possibility and as an absolute reality expands and intensifies our loving.

Thus, this book about death and dying is also a book of life, living and loving. For as we walk through the valley of the shadow, we experience the presence of the Light.

Specifically, this study intends to:

1. Present an overview of the subject of thanatology to provide perspectives for understanding the complexity of death and dying.

2. Describe the dying person's attitudes, expectations and behavior to better understand and care for the dying.

3. Offer guidelines for care of the dying.

4. Help the dying, the loved ones and the caretakers deal with the stresses of dying.

5. Increase awareness of the dynamics and dimensions of grief and assist persons to cope with grief.

6. Inform and reinforce faith. Provide possibilities for hope.

7. Help children, parents and teachers to cope with present and future death-related anxieties and concerns.

8. Furnish information on resources, persons, organizations and materials for reference, research and referral.

9. Discuss some of the main moral and ethical issues which confront those involved in the dying process.

This study approaches the subject of death and dying holistically. This means that the death experience is seen as involving the whole person — body, mind, emotions and spirit. This approach determines and explains the nature and scope of the study. Although much of the material in this book is oriented toward nurses, who are the single group most likely to be present at institutionalized dying common in our society today, the information herein is relevant for everyone.

The thoughts in this book are an accumulation of studies and of personal and professional experiences of the author who, over a period of forty years, has at various times served as a hospital corpsman in the United States Navy, pastor, hospital chaplain, college teacher and chaplain, author and counselor in the field of death and dying. The experiences which some 5,000 nurses from all over our nation have shared in death and dying seminars conducted by the author in the last two years provide a valuable source of information for this book. Their insights, many of which are included, make this study experiential, practical, relevant and contemporary for us all.

Louis Richard Batzler
Frederick, Maryland
May, 1983

*Death is not extinguishing the Light*
*It is putting out the Lamp*
*Because the Dawn has come.*

Rabindranath Tagore

*When you were born you cried*
*And the whole world rejoiced.*
*Live such a life that when you die*
*The whole world cries and you rejoice.*

Traditional Indian saying

*Like a day well spent bestows pleasant sleep*
*So a life well used bestows pleasant death.*

Leonardo da Vinci

*O Lord, may the end of my life be the best of it, may*
*my closing acts be my best acts, and may the best of my*
*days be the day when I shall meet Thee.*

Islamic Prayer

# Introduction

When considering the dying person, there are several basic facts that need to be understood.

1. Dying persons often exhibit attitudes and responses in their dying similar to those attitudes and responses they expressed in their life. Thus each person dies in his or her own way. Each death is unique. Therefore, you cannot construct a "right way to die." This means that attention is to be given to the person rather than to rigid processes and that personal variables will always be present in the dying.

2. It is important to consider where the dying person is in terms of his life cycle. A five-year-old child will manifest attitudes and behavior much different from the ninety-year-old nursing home person. The age of the dying person often involves the psychological maturity, coping mechanisms, frames of reference — all of which influence attitudes and behavior.

3. The causative factors in dying must be considered. Accidents, infections, malformations, metabolic diseases, cancers, organ transplants, amputations, sudden infant death, etc., all have their specific dynamics.

4. The context of dying influences attitudes, behavior and care. These contexts include intensive, emergency, chronic, terminal and recovery care.

5. Dying usually involves relationships and interactions with many persons. The realization of this truth is important in coping with the stresses of the dying and their loved ones.

6. What a dying person needs most is sensitive and caring persons. Caretakers and family members need to realize, however, that their attitudes toward the dying can be a mixture of love and hate. The dying person evokes not only feelings of love and compassion, but also feelings of anger, frustration, disappointment, even hatred. Your awareness of this ambivalence and your ability to accept and tolerate these opposite feelings will help you and the dying.

7. A dying person knows preconsciously that he is dying, even though he may not articulate this awareness to anyone.

8. Dying involves the entire person — body, mind, emotions, spirit. Often as the body becomes weaker, the other aspects of the person need more attention. This is also true for the survivors during the dying of their loved one. A holistic approach to the care of the dying and their loved ones is the most effective and realistic approach for enabling one to die an integrated or a "good death."

An integrated dying involves the person's

a. handling the initial crisis, which comes with the knowledge of impending death, without falling apart.

b. being able to reconcile his life as it now is with goals, plans and dreams that will not be fulfilled.

c. maintaining, even strengthening, relationships with loved ones, and experiencing the healing of long-standing conflicts.

d. being able to separate gradually from loved ones, especially without guilt feelings.

e. working through various episodes of anticipatory grief.

f. separating from important things and arranging for the disposition of possessions.

g. expressing a firm faith in God's love and wisdom which includes a positive attitude concerning the afterlife.

h. being at peace with God, others and self.

*Death does not visit more than once.*
*Be prepared, therefore, for its coming.*

Johann Wolfgang von Goethe

*It is hard to have patience with people who say, "There is no death" or "death doesn't matter." There is death, and whatever happens has consequences, and it and they are irrevocable and irreversible. You might as well say that birth doesn't matter. I look up at the night sky. Is anything more certain than that in all those vast times and spaces, if I was allowed to search them, I should nowhere find her face, her voice, her touch? She died. She is dead. Is the word so difficult to learn?*

C. S. Lewis

*As death is — to be exact — the true goal of life I familiarized myself during the last couple of years to such an extent with this true and best friend of man, that its image contains nothing terrifying but, on the contrary, much which is appeasing and consoling. Thanks be to God that he granted me the good fortune to have had the opportunity to learn and understand death as the key to our true happiness. I never go to bed without thinking — regardless of my youth — it might be possible that I will no longer be alive on the following day. But, just the same, none of my many acquaintances would call me sad, or ill-tempered. Every single day I give thanks to my Creator for this happiness, and I wish with all my heart that other people will have it too.*

Wolfgang A. Mozart

# Chapter 1
# Thanatology

Within the last seventy-five years the human race has produced more scientists than in all of previous human history. The results of this phenomenon are evident in the physical, natural and social sciences. Fantastic achievements in communication, transportation, biochemistry, medicine, food production, construction technology, electronics, computerization, psychotherapies, government and community organization, and many others, attest to mankind's marvelous skills, imagination and evolving consciousness.

One aspect of these accomplishments is the emergence of a new consciousness and new approaches to death, dying and life after death. If you examine carefully the literature on this subject and observe the increasing involvement of some segments of our society in death, you will readily see significant changes in dealing with the dying. These changes have come about not only because of scientific and technological advances, but also because of changes in mores, moralities and modes of living.

Some of the most valuable contributions toward understanding and coping with the dynamics and dimensions of death have come from the discipline of thanatology, the formal study of death. Thanatology is an art and a science. As an art, it stresses humanistic approaches to dying and bereavement, and as a science thanatology emphasizes the need for death education, systematic investigation and inquiry. The number of thanatologists increases each year, courses in thanatology are now being taught in colleges and universities,[1] abbreviated courses are appearing in high schools, nursing and medical schools, and a few schools are offering graduate work in the subject.[2] Seminars and workshops on death and dying are being held throughout the country. Organizations, books, and periodicals are bringing new insights and perspectives to the subject.[3] Death is being brought out of the grave.

The scope of thanatology reveals the complexity of death and dying in our day. A syllabus of a course in thanatology might include the following.

PERSONAL REACTIONS TO DEATH
Feelings, attitudes — denying, defying, desiring, preoccupation, accepting, integrating.

WAYS OF DEATH
Heart attack, terminal illness, old age, malnutrition and starvation, accidents and acts of nature, psychological causes, suicide, war, domestic violence, genocide, assassination, execution, homicide, martyrdom, crib deaths, etc.

BIOCHEMICAL PROCESS
Dying, at death, after death.

PSYCHOLOGY OF DEATH AND DYING
Life goals, fear, existential dread, meaninglessness, guilt, stages (denial, anger, bargaining,

depression, acceptance), grief, reactions of terminally ill according to life period (childhood, teen-age, adult, aged), mourning, and ritualization, bereavement, counseling.

## CLINICAL MANAGEMENT
Physician and nursing care in hospital and home, keeping patient alive, organ transplants, pain management, comatose states, ethical problems, autopsy, organ donations.

## FUNERAL
Rites and practices, funeral service, costs, memorialization, disposal of body.

## LEGAL PROBLEMS
Legal definitions, abortion, euthanasia, wills, estates, life insurance, death benefits.

## ECOLOGICAL, POLITICAL, DEMOGRAPHIC ASPECTS OF DEATH
Overpopulation, population control, ecological suicide (pollution), starvation, war, genocide.

## CULTURAL VIEWS OF DEATH
Eastern and western views of death, American Indian views, other.

## RELIGIOUS PERSPECTIVES ON DEATH
Ancient and modern religious views, major world religious views, spiritual death, karma, satori, soul in afterlife, identity, judgment, heaven, hell, prayers for the dead, communication with the departed, reincarnation, resurrection.

## PARAPSYCHOLOGICAL VIEWS OF DEATH
Physical, etheric and spiritual bodies, spiritual

spheres, progression, growth, premonition and predestination, survival, ghosts, visions, voices, apparitions, mediumship, dreams, out-of-body experiences, rescue work.

## PHILOSOPHICAL PERSPECTIVES ON DEATH
Eternal life, immortality, survival, arguments for survival (analogical, ethical, teleological, revelation, resurrection, justice, moral, character of God, psychical phenomena, conservation).

## DEATH IN THE ARTS
Music, painting, photography, sculpture, literature, drama.

## DEATH EDUCATION
For children, school curricula, religious education, mass media.

This abbreviated syllabus provides an overview of death and dying, shows the democracy of death, indicates that death is for all seasons and ages and that the issue is relevant and significant for everyone.

*If there is one preoccupation that colors society most pervasively, it's fear of death. That has to do with war, it has to do with economics, it has to do with style of living, it has to do with leaving institutions behind, with wills, it has to do with being so much of people's consciousness all the time. The minute you can focus directly on that, the minute you are not afraid of death and you can convey your non-fear of death to the culture, the whole game starts to flip around. That's why I really see that consciousness is much more a major social change agent than say, politics. Politics is merely a perpetuation of the existing myth — it's more like revolution, it's not like evolution. We have the possibility of evolution but it lies within each human heart, it's not something that you can socially institutionalize. You can't have a group of conscious healers institutionalized. You can merely see each healer as an individual who must accept responsibility for their own work. That's important. To me, the only interesting social institution is the individual human heart. All the rest of them are creations of human mind — they come and they go.*

Ram Dass

# Chapter 2
# Death and Dying
# in America

The various attitudes that Americans have toward death (denying, defying, desiring, preoccupied,[1] accepting, integrating) help you to see something of the ambivalence and confusion which exists toward death in this country. This ambivalence and confusion is seen in the "awe of death and an attraction to death; risking death and loving life; wanting happiness and behaving in self-destructive ways; regarding death as taboo and insisting on new permissiveness to talk about it; an obsession with The Bomb and a deep concern with spiritual rebirth."[2]

Ambivalence and confusion also stem from significant changes in the causes of death, the increased exposure to death and dying and the kinds of care given to the dying within the last seventy-five years. These changes include:

1. A significant shift in the mortality rates according to age. Years ago about two-thirds of the deaths in America were those of children under fifteen. With the progress made in conquering most of the fatal childhood diseases, this number has been significantly reduced. Now the majority of persons who die are over fifty.

2. Today, three-quarters of the Americans who die do so in institutions — hospitals, nursing

homes, mental institutions, prisons. This institutionalization of dying has a number of important ramifications and complications for families and health-care professionals.

3. The media has brought death and dying into our midst in a number of ways. We see mass death in holocausts, famine, war, refugees right in our living room on the television. The death theme, like the sex theme, is now being used more often by businesses to sell products. These more frequent exposures, blatant and subtle, affect our sensibilities and attitudes.

4. The causes of death have increased in number and kind. Accidents, homicide, suicide bring death more into our everyday living in traumatic ways.

5. Care for the dying is now mostly done by professionals — doctors, nurses, clergy, various therapists — which lessens some of the painful and difficult experiences in dealing with the dying, but which also creates psychological and spiritual dilemmas for the dying person and the loved ones.

6. The erosion of religious faith in many persons poses new problems. For the faithful, death usually means a transition to a more glorious existence. For those who have little or no religious faith, death is more of an end, a movement toward non-being. This latter attitude can cause serious problems as the person undergoes the dying process. The absence of faith is frequently associated with a loss or diminishing of one's

identity or selfhood (we know who we are when we know whose we are) which also creates problems even before one enters his dying phase.

7. The great achievements of medical technology have done much to prolong and sustain life. The sustaining of life, even when the life is virtually gone, has created many bioethical and legal difficulties as well as the anguishing problems of indecision, guilt, enormous expense and freedom of choice.

8. The complexity of death and dying in our day is seen in the number of ways death is defined.

    a. Medical or clinical death in which vital signs are absent and the person no longer functions. The term clinical death is also being used to describe "reversible" death in which a person is resuscitated after a short time.

    b. Biological death is the cessation of organ and tissue function.

    c. Cellular death.

    d. Cerebral death indicates the end of cerebral cortex functions.

    e. Brain death includes cessation of entire brain and brain stem functions.

    f. Legal death refers to the termination of the legal existence and, therefore, rights of a person.

    g. Spiritual death indicates departure of soul from body or the death of the soul.

These changes and the resultant ambivalence and confusion about death and dying point to the need for serious, careful research, well-conceived and carried-out educational programs, proper care and counseling not only for the comfort of the dying and their loved ones, but also for the well-being of our total society. To learn about death and dying is to learn about living. To respect and lovingly care for the dying is to respect and lovingly care for the living. Pain and suffering teach us compassion and patience. Sorrow and grief help us to experience joy. To squarely and intelligently face death, is to openly face life with all of its privileges, possibilities, opportunities and challenges. Most Americans today still have much to learn about these blessings that come from the dying.

*I know not what the future hath*
*Of marvel or surprise,*
*Assured alone that life and death*
*His mercy underlies.*

John Greenleaf Whittier

*There is always going to be suffering as long as you*
*are attached to something that is changing.*

Ram Dass

*When through the deep waters I call thee to go,*
*The rivers of sorrow shall not overflow;*
*For I will be with thee thy troubles to bless,*
*And sanctify to thee thy deepest distress.*

Anonymous

*In death, as in an ocean, all our slow or swift di-*
*minishments flow out and merge. Death is the sum and*
*consummation of our diminishments. . . .*
*The function of death is to provide the necessary*
*entrace into our inmost selves.*

Pierre Teilhard de Chardin

# Chapter 3
# The Dying Person

The many factors in the dying process show that there are no easy answers in caring for the dying, no precise processes or set stages that can be forecast, no rigid guidelines to follow. Each person dies uniquely. However, there are some common denominators in persons' attitudes and behavior and if you can be aware of why these attitudes and behaviors exist, then you can offer better care. To know the "why" is a great help in knowing the "how." One way to ascertain the "why" is to look at the changes dying persons undergo, especially if they are dying in an institutional setting. These changes are primarily ones of separation and loss. The diagram below clearly reveals the traumatic changes most dying persons experience. The circle represents the dying person and each segment indicates the person's deprivations, losses, separations, divestments. The accumulation of these significant changes clearly reveals the extreme stresses that the dying and their loved ones undergo and, therefore, why they behave in certain ways.

Some of these losses can also be considered gains, e.g., faith, hope, meaning, but these gains are usually associated with a dimension of life beyond this one. Also, as these changes accumulate, the dying often experience a new consciousness which includes clarification of values, the increase of intuitive awareness, healing of broken relationships, being more in touch with oneself and a sense of peace and joy that passes all understanding. Thus, not all of the changes that the dying undergo are negative. In addition, the dying person may express a deep love and concern for others, an openness and new courage so as to no longer be bothered by what others think, an unusual enthusiasm, elimination of some long-standing negative forces, less concern about money, material things or personal neatness, and a winsome wisdom and wholeness. A person who evinces these attitudes and behaviors teaches us much about life and usually dies a beautiful death.

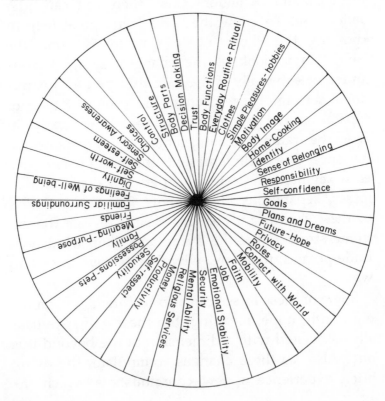

Dr. Irvin Yalom, in his work with terminally ill cancer patients, notes the "personal growth" in terms of

A rearrangement of life's priorities; a trivializing of the trivial

A sense of liberation: being able to choose not to do those things that they do not wish to do

An enhanced sense of living in the immediate present, rather than postponing life until retirement or some other point in the future

A vivid appreciation of the elemental facts of life: the changing seasons, the wind, falling leaves, the last Christmas, and so forth

Deeper communication with loved ones than before the crisis

Fewer interpersonal fears, less concern about rejection, greater willingness to take risks, than before the crisis.[1]

These inner changes and new values, perspectives and priorities emphasize the importance of open and honest communication with the dying patient.

*The last of human freedoms — to choose one's attitude in any given set of circumstances.*

Viktor Frankl

*Do not go gentle into that good night, . . .*
*Rage, rage, against the dying of the light.*

Dylan Thomas

*Thus it is observed, that men sometimes, upon the hour of their departure, do speak and reason above themselves; for then the soul, beginning to be freed from the ligaments of the body, begins to reason like her self, and to discourse in a strain above mortality.*

Religio Medici

*Life and death are not two opposed forces; they are simply two ways of looking at the same force.*

Johann Wolfgang von Goethe

# Chapter 4
# Attitudes and Responses of the Dying

Death and life are inseparable companions. Therefore, in seeking to cope with persons' attitudes and responses in their dying, it is important to know something about their life. This knowing enables the caretaker to foster trust, help the dying maintain or regain their identity, allow the dying and the family to better cope with episodes of anticipatory grief, facilitate communication and openness and create a loving atmosphere which is so essential for the dying.

The chart below presents some of the probabilities of the dying person's attitudes and responses. Not all dying persons go through all of these stages, nor do they necessarily experience them in the order noted. The intensity, movement and duration of these stages are influenced by factors such as the person's psychological maturity, the coping techniques available, various frames of reference (religion, sex, age), the severity and the progress of the disease, the attitudes of doctors, nurses, family, friends and any other support persons, and where the person is in his living-dying interval.

The living-dying interval is the period between the "crisis-knowledge of death" and the "point of death." It can be divided into three clinical phases:

# Attitudes and Responses of the Dying

| Ego levels and activity | Emotional response | Self-awareness and self-determination |
|---|---|---|
| | **SHOCK** | |
| **UNREAL** | **DENIAL** | **EXCITEMENT** |
| I pretend nothing has happened. | I can't believe it. Not me. | A new chapter in my life is beginning. |
| **RESENTMENT** | **ANGER** | **HOLDING ON** |
| I resent this dirty deal life is giving me. | Damn that disease, that doctor. I hate you. Why me, God? Why now? | I am going to hold onto the past. |
| **FEAR** | **BARGAINING** | **HOLDING BACK** |
| I'm afraid. It's my fault. I should have been a better person. | There must be some way to beat this — prayer, medicine, doctors. | I will hold back my real feeling in my fear of living this way. |
| | **EMPTINESS** | **ANTICIPATORY** |
| **DISINTEGRATION** | **DEPRESSION** | **GRIEF** |
| Who am I? I am disappearing. | There is no use in going on. | I grieve over the losses I now experience. |
| | **ACCEPTANCE** | |
| **REINTEGRATION** | **HOPE** | **RENEWAL** |
| I'm coming alive in a new way. | I am really sick but I still have hope. Miracles happen. | I am becoming a new being in new relationships and new values. |

With certain modifications, this information is applicable to persons who experience severe losses of almost any kind.

1. the acute crisis phase, 2. the chronic living-dying phase, and 3. the terminal phase. Each phase has its own dynamics which influence patient responses.[1]

Denial is a much-used defense by the dying and it is not always negative or disintegrating. Denial has many expressions and levels. They include *existential denial* which relates to one's mortality. It is a fundamental denial used by all persons at various times during their life. *Psychological denial* is that defense mechanism whereby one represses the known facts. This might include repudiation and rationalization. *Nonattention denial* is shifting of awareness and attention elsewhere, focusing on other facts and factors.

Denial in death situations is used by patients, caretakers and families. Examples abound.

> One family, informed by emergency room personnel that a son had been killed, came in the next day with new clothes for him to wear home that day. Another family, a member of which had died and been cremated, did not pick up his belongings or the ashes.

> One dying teen-ager, whose body was wasting away through his illness, pasted pictures of himself, as he was when well, on the hospital wall. This denial was a source of strength for him. One clergyman was confronted by a grieving son, whose mother had died, with the mandate to raise her from the dead on the day of burial.

Each of these cases exemplify the many ways persons use denial, sometimes very bizarre. Often you find it is the family and staff who need help in their denials rather than the dying person.

Anger also has many faces and is an emotion that virtually all dying persons experience. Anger is that emotion that seeks to prevent change in one's situation, to hold on to that which one has and enjoys. A dying person's anger may manifest in violence or in withdrawal and becoming mute. Families, too, experience various levels of anger as they undergo the separations and losses. It is important to realize that this is a normal reaction and that, in most cases, the anger is not directed personally at the caretaker.

Depression is a complex state which the dying and those who care for the dying experience. Depression in the dying is primarily due to the accumulation of factors involved in the dying process and, as such, is very difficult to deal with. Many painful emotional responses emerge in the depressive state. Professional therapy, including medication, is sometimes necessary. Continued compassionate and loving presence is most important.

Most dying persons have hope for their recovery even though they may not always overtly express that hope. However, as the end draws near, some persons exchange their hope for healing in this life for a hope in the next life. This change in consciousness is usually observable and offers the opportunity for family and caretakers to nurture this dimension of the dying person's life. Clergy can be helpful at this time.

*Death in itself is nothing; but we fear*
*To be we know not what, we know not where.*

John Dryden

*To fear death, gentlemen, is nothing other than to*
*think oneself wise when one is not; for it is to think one*
*knows what one does not know. No man knows*
*whether death may not even turn out to be the greatest*
*of blessings for a human being and yet people fear it as*
*if they know for certain. That is the greatest of evils.*

Socrates

*When pain is to be borne a little courage helps more*
*than much knowledge, a little human sympathy more*
*than much courage and the least tincture of the love of*
*God more than all.*

C. S. Lewis

*Teach me your mood, O patient stars!*
*Who climb each night the ancient sky*
*Leaving on space no shade, no scars,*
*No trace of age, no fear to die.*

Ralph Waldo Emerson

*Death causes us to lose our footing completely in our-*
*selves so as to deliver us over to the powers of heaven*
*and earth. This is its final terror — but it is also, for the*
*mystic, the climax of his bliss; it is our final entry, there*
*to remain forever, into the milieu that dominates, that*
*carries us off, that consumes.*

Pierre Teilhard de Chardin

# Chapter 5

# Dying Persons' Fears

Fear is a major emotion of dying persons. Fears can be classified according to 1. the dying process, 2. relationships, and 3. being or existence. The fears involved in the process of dying have a number of motivators such as those of pain, suffering, changes in body, sorrow, loss of self-control. In relationships, fears center around the questions of separations, what will happen to the surviving loved ones, how they will respond to the person's death and deal with their grief. The fears associated with being involve the concerns about ceasing to be, loss of identity, what happens after death. These fears are usually more difficult to ascertain or surface, but they are real. They also include questions about the meaning and purpose of life, guilt and what will be missed in living.

1. *Fears related to the process of dying*

    a. Suffering and pain

        Most persons, whether they are dying or not, fear pain and suffering. Physical, mental and emotional pain for the dying is usually heightened because the pain is identified with the dying process. Pain-killing medication, though helpful and often necessary, is not the total answer to the relief or fear of pain. One's self-awareness, understanding and attitude are important factors in pain management. Pain that has no meaning, no location or no explanation usually becomes more severe. The unknown and unmanageable elements in pain tend to increase fears and the intensity of pain. If pain is identified with punishment, isolation or rejection, the suffering can be almost unbearable. Professional therapy or compassionate and understanding loved ones can be helpful in such cases. Other pain relief possibilities can also be utilized in place of or in addition to medication. Numerous successes have been achieved through such techniques as biofeedback, in which the person learns to monitor and diminish or control his own pain, acupuncture, hypnosis and reflexology.

Although it is important to have the dying patient as pain free and as comfortable as possible, you need to be careful about over-sedation, not only from a physiological point of view, but also from a psychological standpoint. Dying is a most important experience in the person's life and it is well, in most cases, that the person be conscious as much as possible. It is at the moment of death that something super-significant can happen for the dying one as well as for the survivors standing by.

b. Loss of self-control

Loss of self-control leads to the loss of self. This fear is partly culturally motivated. In our society where self-control, self-determination, decisiveness, rationality, goal-setting, achievement and success are so important, the loss of any of these controls is often considered a diminution or even a loss of self. The loss of physical mobility, vitality, energy and strength increases this fear and the person feels a threat to his ego and integrity. The fear of loss of self-control may be expressed in a person's dread of losing consciousness through anesthesia or heavy sedation and fear of suffocation — the loss of breath is related to the loss of life. Insomnia sometimes is associated with this fear.

An important challenge for the caretaker is to facilitate and to encourage the dying to maintain, or regain, as much control and authority as possible in daily tasks, choices and decisions, while, at the same time, avoiding any criticism, shaming, blaming or impatience for failure of a person's control capabilities.

c. Loss of body parts

In addition to the pain which accompanies disfigurement and losses in the body, there is the mental and emotional pain that occurs. There is often a chain reaction which is involved in this fear.

The sense of shame, disgrace, inadequacy, embarassment brings out fears of being ridiculed, rejected, isolated, and the resultant loss of self-esteem and self-integrity. Where major parts of the body are lost, the dying person may even question his identity. This fear is especially prevalent in the chronically dying. Recognizing this fear and the related feelings and attitudes, can help the caretaker in deciding the best care. Compassionate acceptance of the patient, however he appears or acts, affirming his personhood and being present are all important.

d. Sorrow and grief

The actual and potential losses that the dying person faces are many and intense. Each loss brings with it some sorrow and grief. A primary task for the caretaker is to help prevent the person from being overwhelmed with sorrow and grief. This can be done by dealing with the grief episodes as they occur, providing opportunities for those pleasures, satisfactions, and achievements still available and normalizing life as much as possible.

2. *Fears involving relationships*

a. Loss of family and friends

Because relationships with loved ones involve so many aspects of one's total self (physical contact, emotional ties, spiritual journeys), the fear of loss and separation is intense. For both the dying person and the family, it is important to engage in anticipatory grief work. Some cultures, aware of the significance of this fear, have incorporated into their family and social life customs, rituals and feasts of separation. To work through the grief of separation before death, can heal many long-standing wounds, clarify, confirm and settle important matters pertaining to the well-being (material and non-material) of the survivors, and help assuage the emotions of anger, guilt and resentment. Sometimes professional intervention is required.

b. Being a bother

Many dying persons, concerned about their loved ones, have a fear of being a bother, a nuisance or imposition. This fear might be related, in part, to the possible anger of the family. Usually support persons outside of the family can be helpful in alleviating this fear.

c. Loneliness

The fear of loneliness has many faces. Feeling deserted, physically isolated, abandoned, ignored, or rejected all contribute to this fear. Even if these feelings don't surface, they are ever-present possibilities for the dying. Since three-quarters of those who die do so in hospitals, nursing homes and mental institutions, this poses a challenge and places additional responsibility for the dying on the professional caretaker. Most hospitals and staffs are conceived to provide acute remedial care — to cure — and, therefore, are neither physically nor psychologically oriented to really care for the dying.

The hospice movement is one answer to this dilemma, but there still needs to be more consciousness of caring and compassion for the dying in institutions. This requires much interdisciplinary cooperation, advocacy and courage on the part of all who serve in this capacity. It is encouraging to note that some hospitals are sending more nurses for death and dying courses, conducting in-house seminars, and having staff meetings dealing with the dynamics, dimensions and dilemmas of death and dying.

3. *Fears relating to being and existence*

　a. Ceasing to be

Underlying all of the other fears is the fear of non-being. Extinction, selflessness, non-being are basic anxieties, which, for the dying, become up-front, acute, existential fears. Nothingness and dissolution are antagonistic to the human body, mind and spirit. The so-called death agonies may be related to this fear of regression into nothingness. Also, this may explain the special fear, restlessness and insomnia that dying patients exhibit at night or in the dark.[1] This fear emphasizes the importance of frequently being present with the dying and also being open to sharing in their spiritual journey.

b. Loss of identity

The quest and struggle to attain and maintain identity begins shortly after birth. Self-consciousness, self-determination and self-transcendence represent stages in the growth of the individual and in the development of identity and personhood. Identity is that which speaks not only of uniqueness, individuality and integrity, but also of community and relationships. Each person is a part *from* humanity and a part *of* humanity. It is the interaction of these participations that fashions one's identity.

The loss of identity signals the loss of selfhood, of meaning, of accomplishment, of worth. The dying are especially vulnerable to this loss and, therefore, the fear is great. To help the dying person cope with this fear, it is important to recognize the formative forces in creating and maintaining identity and to facilitate the continuance of these. This includes maintaining contact with the familiar, affirming the beauty and value of the continuity of life through family, friends and achievements. In the spiritual context, it means fostering faith in the continuance of life beyond death.

c. Unknown

Fear of the unknown persists throughout life. This fear usually is proportionate to the degree of danger involved and to the extent which the unknown is not knowable. For the dying, this fear is usually intense because of the number of unknowns and of the great unknown beyond death. Such questions as what changes will occur in my body, how will my family and friends respond to my dying, what will happen to them, what of my plans, projects and goals, what expenses will be involved — all of these plague the patient.

This fear is also heightened by the many information inputs that the person receives and which often cause consternation and confusion.

These include

1. Direct statements from the physician.
2. Overheard comments of physician to others.
3. Direct statements from other personnel, including aides, nurses, technologists.
4. Overheard comments by staff to each other.
5. Direct statements from family, friends, clergy, lawyer.
6. Changes in the behavior of others toward the patient.
7. Changes in medical care routines, procedures, medications.
8. Changes in physical location.

9. Self-diagnosis, including reading of medical books, records and charts.
10. Signals from the body and changes in physical status.
11. Altered responses by others toward the future.

All concerned with the dying can have a part in helping the person in this fear through open, honest, and clear communication.

d. What happens to me after death

This question usually arises in childhood, especially if the child experiences the death of a loved one. The question is translated into a fear as persons approach death. This fear may not always be verbalized, but it is present. Any answers you can give from your own studies and experience plus reassurances of your continual love and presence — your not forsaking nor forgetting — are helpful.

*Certain is death for the born,*
*And certain is birth for the dead.*
*When one is born, death follows.*
*When one dies, rebirth follows.*

Bhagavad Gita

*We fear death for no good reason. Even if we fear*
*death, we are going to die anyway, so why not accept it*
*with courage? If a person is brave in the face of death,*
*then when he is dying he feels that he is just going to*
*sleep.He feels no torment.*

Swami Muktananda

*No atom of matter in the whole vastness of the uni-*
*verse is lost. How then can man's soul, which comprises*
*the whole world in one idea, be lost?*

The Talmud

*I am a soul. I know well that what I render up to the*
*grave is not myself. That which is myself will go*
*elsewhere. The whole creation is perpetual ascension,*
*brute to man, man to God. To divest ourselves more and*
*more of matter, to be clothed more and more with spirit,*
*such is the law.*

Victor Hugo

*Death stands above me, whispering low*
*I know not what into my ear;*
*Of his strange language all I know,*
*There is no word of fear.*

Walter Savage Landor

# Chapter 6
# Alleviating Fears

The type, intensity and duration of fears of the dying vary. Such factors as belief systems, severity of pain and disease, medications, attitudes of caretakers and family, and pain threshold all influence the person's dealing with his fears.

The following are ways to help alleviate fears.

1. Trying different pain management techniques such as biofeedback, hypnosis, reflexology, relaxation, humor.

2. Providing clear, honest information and communication to lessen the fear of pain and the unknown.

3. Being aware of and dealing with the factors of guilt and punishment as a cause of pain and reason for the person's illness.

4. Enabling persons to maintain control and authority as much as possible.

5. Understanding and being compassionate concerning the fears of loss of body parts.

6. Confronting the fears associated with aniticipatory grief and sorrow when they appear and providing opportunities for satisfying accomplishments.

7. Establishing trustful and meaningful relationships with the dying and being a frequent and loving presence.

8. Nurturing faith, when indicated, which might include prayer, affirming the power, presence and love of God, and the reality of life after death.

9. Helping person maintain contact with the familiar and providing continuity of life experiences, especially the positive, through family and friends.

10. Affirming value and meaning in the life of the dying person and helping the person to be aware of having accomplished something worthwhile in life.

11. Keeping hope alive, even while accepting the reality of impending death.

12. Helping the person to see his living and dying as part of a larger plan in the nature of the universe in which he has had and will continue to have a part.

13. Patiently accepting the person's denial of death, repression of feelings and his minimizing the seriousness of his condition.

Other more philosophical and long-range methods for alleviating the fear of death are ignoring death; occupying our minds with "positive" emotions such as contemplation on nature, love of God; facing the prospect of death; "familiarizing" oneself with death; "minimizing" death; combining "minimizing" and "familiarizing"; setting a just value on life; becoming detached from worldly things; denying self and living for others; affirming death as a higher state of life rather than as annihilation; having a consciousness of having accomplished something outstanding; leading a rich and full life.[1]

*But cure without care makes us into rulers, controllers, manipulators and prevents a real community from taking shape. Cure without care makes us preoccupied with quick changes, impatient and unwilling to share each other's burden. And so cure can often become offending instead of liberating. It is therefore not so strange that cure is not seldom refused by people in need.*

Henri Nouwen


*We've got the wrong focus; we're still focusing on the technique rather than the quality of the being who is using the technique, who is recipient, and the conditions under which the technique is being used.*

Ram Dass


*I am not the brood of the dust and sod,*
*Nor a shuttled thread in the loom of fate;*
*But the child divine of the living God,*
*With eternity for my life's estate.*
*I am not a sport of a cosmic night,*
*Nor a thing of chance that has grown to man;*
*But a deathless soul on my upward flight,*
*And my Father's heir in His wondrous plan.*

A. Romanes


*My friends are lazy today, considering the fact that I'm dying – they might have sent a card.*

Rudyard Kipling

# Chapter 7

# Expectations and Wishes of the Dying

There are many different dynamics in the stages that the dying go through. This means that care for the dying is multi-faceted. The dying often voice their expectations and wishes concerning their care and these provide valuable information for caretakers.

The following expectations and wishes are those which most dying persons affirm. Of course, not all dying persons necessarily have all of these expectations and wishes, nor do all dying persons affirm them with the same intensity or frequency.

1. *To be treated as a living human being until death.*

This expectation may sound strange, yet if you consider how many persons, including caretakers, respond negatively to the dying, you can understand the validity of this concern. The dying person is frequently isolated and avoided in institutions and homes. Conversation with the dying is often trivial, the attitude of family, physician, clergy or nurse is often non-commital or even that of denial, the environment is hush-hush, dark and foreboding.

Two acute anxieties of the dying are loss of identity and loss of self-worth. Anything that can be done to affirm and enhance the dying person's identity and personhood (e.g., calling by name, touching, listening, reminiscing) is valuable. Frequent contact, judicious use of humor, continuity of care, honesty, giving opportunity for choices and control, creating as pleasant and as normal an environment as possible, being in touch with your own feelings about death and, above all, compassion — all of these can help the dying person feel human and maintain dignity.

2. *To maintain hope and have those who care for me also maintain a sense of hopefulness.*

This desire is a difficult one to fulfill for the dying person and caretakers. There is a delicate balance between the impending fatal reality and the hope for recovery, and that balance constantly shifts as the patient receives new information and/or experiences body changes, treatments, or movement to new locations. Hope for the dying has two dimensions. The one is the hope that the patient will miraculously recover, which sometimes does happen. The other hope is that of a more glorious life after death. Although these two hopes seem contradictory, it is possible to hold them in a creative tension without destroying either. The one hope is based on the will to live here and now; the other on the faith that death is a transition to another form of life there and then. Hope in either case is clearly related to and nurtured by faith and love — faith in and love for God and those who work for a cure.

3. *To have my questions answered clearly and honestly and to not be deceived by anyone who cares for me.*

This is one of the most frequent and frustrating expectations. It is traumatic and tragic to see how often relationships, which have been open and honest during one's lifetime, become closed and dishonest during one's dying. There are many reasons for this. Physical and emotional pain, anger and guilt can distort, intentionally or unintentionally, the truth. Fear frequently fosters falsehood; the sense of failure and inadequacy can promote dishonesty; inability of caretakers and loved ones to face their own death prevents or delays truth-telling. The excuses and reasons that persons give for not being honest with the dying are endless.

Open communication with the dying is a special problem for nurses who usually are the primary caretakers. Often nurses need to adjust their involvement and communication with the dying person according to many pressures — person's awareness of his condition, family's and/or physician's denial and instructions not to tell, and the internal emotional stresses of the nurse. The dilemmas include 1. the nurse's knowing that the person is dying, but the person has not been told; 2. the person suspects, but has not been told; 3. both the person and nurse know, but do not talk about it; 4. both person and nurse know and acknowledge it as such.[1]

Nurses, or any caretakers, should not force a dying person to talk about his death.

The main question about telling a person he is dying is not whether to tell or not to tell, but who should tell, how much, what, how, when and how often.

a. The physician has the primary responsibility to tell.

b. It is usually best to tell only as much as the dying person can use and absorb at the moment. Giving information gradually is generally most helpful for all concerned.

c. The substance of the information given should include the physician's findings and the treatment planned. Assurance needs to be given that the person will not be abandoned.

d. The manner of telling will vary greatly and has important implications. The predominant concerns of the dying are not facts as much as fears of isolation, pain, abandonment or being sent to a nursing home. Simple sincerity is better than cliches or standard formulas.

e. The dying know preconsciously that they are dying. Deceit or dissimulation risks alienation and distrust. Therefore, information should be given as soon as possible.

f. Frequency of information will depend on the dying person's questions and attitudes as well as his trust in the caretakers.[2]

Although honesty is the best policy, caretakers should strive to be honest in such a way that the truth is most constructive or least destructive. Gentleness and timing are important. Hope should not be immediately squelched, yet the seriousness of the situation should not be minimized. Assurances need to be given that all possible support systems and staff will be utilized. Genuine and firm love is essential.

4. *To participate in decisions concerning my care.*

Dying persons face the loss of control in almost every area of their lives. To lose control over your life is to lose your selfhood. It is very important to help the dying maintain as much control over their life as possible. This involves giving persons opportunities for choices and decision-making even if these decisions seem small, such as choosing their menu or brushing their teeth. Attending physicians, family members and nurses can be instrumental in meeting this desire of patients. Institutional regulations that restrict decision-making by the dying might be re-examined and challenged.

A prime task of the caretaker is to provide dying persons an environment in which they can be free. This means creating a space in which the individual has the optimum freedom to make choices such as how much and how they want to work on their body, or have their body worked on and which religious or philosophical system they wish to embrace and work with.

Some nurses have stated that their advocacy for the dying is affecting changes in attitudes and regulations of hospital administrators. These changes include recognition of the therapeutic value of open communication with the dying, special staff meetings of nurses, physicians and hospital administrators, in-service training programs, sponsoring of hospice groups, attending death and dying seminars and the use of multidisciplinary approaches to the dying.

5. *To be able to express my feelings about my illness and approaching death.*

This wish emphasizes the value of listening to and empathizing with the dying. You listen with your eyes and heart as well as with your ears. Watch the body language. Real listening is giving a maximum of attention with a minimum of intention, i.e., listening with body, mind and spirit and not letting your own agenda and will get in the way. Too often we hear only what we want to hear. This listening requires patience, openness, gentleness and compassion. To be able to relate positively and creatively to an emotionally expressive person concerning his death requires that the caretaker be in touch with his own death feelings and attitudes.

6. *To have persons involved in my life and dying respect my choices concerning the way I prefer to die and the disposition of my body.*

These two wishes involve a number of complicated issues — euthanasia, the right to die, death with dignity, autopsy, cremation, organ donation, funeral arrangements. The Living Will or a regular will, and such documents as Looking Ahead (see Chapter 14) are ways to help these choices of the person to be honored and carried out. The conflicting wishes of family members, attitudes of the physicians, threats of malpractice suits all contribute to the difficult dilemmas that arise here. Each case has its own uniqueness and needs to be dealt with on that basis. Usually a team approach (physician, family, patient, clergy, therapist) is best when the issue is stalemated.

This wish of the dying person is one that challenges the survivors' and caretakers' respect and love for the dying one. Be careful about your death bed promises. The answers are not easy.

7. *To be free from pain.*

Pain management is a priority for the dying. Pain management is not easy. Too much pain medication can sometimes hasten death, thereby leaving physicians, nurses and hospital administrators open to criticism and suits. Heavy doses of pain medication can so sedate a person that he virtually loses consciousness and contact with reality. This deprives one of an integrated dying experience, of choices and decision-making and of the values that one finds through suffering. Heavy sedation can be a blessing and/or a burden. The diminishing or closing down of communication can deprive dying persons and survivors of meaningful and healing relationships. Pain is one of our greatest gifts and teachers. Much research is being done in pain management and caretakers should be open to discovering and using new techniques which will allow the dying one to be as alert and aware as possible with the minimum of pain. Techniques proving helpful include biofeedback, hypnosis, relaxation and meditation, reflexology, visualization, play therapy, acupuncture, acupressure, music therapy, physical therapy, psychotherapy and specific affirmations.

8. *To have my loved ones receive help (if needed) in dealing with death.*

This wish comes from the compassion of the

dying for their loved ones and the realization that it is often the survivors who have the most difficulty in dealing with death. It is one expression of the dying person's anticipatory grief and can be a most touching and beautiful episode in the dying process.

9. *To share my spiritual concepts and experiences and to receive spiritual nurture from others.*

Although not always overtly articulated, this concern is within the mind and heart of virtually all who are dying. As one moves toward death and is deprived more and more of relationships, things, experiences and opportunities, there is an awakening of the spiritual faculties within. Intuition becomes more sensitive and operative. There is a new face-to-faceness with one's soul, a releasing of spiritual energies that enhance and ennoble life, new interest in what lies beyond death and a hungering for spiritual nurture. The way to truth is through spirit.

This need can be met by many persons — not just religious figures — by sharing one's own faith through scripture, prayer, personal testimony and, most of all, by a deep love from the center of one's being. It is the spiritual quality of love that brings forth life, nurtures and gives life joy and meaning. It is love that finally crowns life as it ends on this plane of existence.

10. *To be cared for by competent and sensitive persons who will seek to understand and help me with my needs and desires.*

During life you wish for the best in whatever

you experience. In dying you wish for the same. The trauma of dying is lessened when you trust the knowledge and skills of caretakers and when caretakers express kindness, love and genuine caring. The dying person is especially delicate, vulnerable and fearful. If both cure (doing to) and care (doing with) are carried out with competency and sensitivity, the person and family will be greatly comforted. Assurance that the best and most are being done for the dying can modify anger, frustration, and despair and help prevent threats of malpractice suits and ease the conscience of those who work for the dying.

11. *To not die alone.*

One of the greatest fears of the person is dying alone. It is also a fear of the loved ones. This explains the person's fear of the dark and of physical isolation in hospital rooms. It is important to have someone present with the dying as much as possible (preferably the closest family member), to touch the person often and to reassure him when leaving that you will return.

12. *To be allowed and helped to live as normally as possible.*

Change carries with it some apprehension and anxiety. The change from a well individual to a sick and dying one is very traumatic. A prime responsibility for caretakers and loved ones is to normalize the dying person's life as much as possible. Even if a person needs to be in an institution when dying, much can be done. Frequent visits, cards, familiar things, continuity of care, explaining routines, discovering and facilitating patient preferences, conversation about the familiar, permitting freedom of movement and allowing choices are ways of meeting this desire.

*I will rejoice that from all tormenting we can retreat always upon the Invisible Heart, upon the Celestial Love, and that not to be soothed merely, but to be replenished, not to be compensated, but to receive power to make all things new.*

Ralph Waldo Emerson


*No being can fall apart into nothingness,*
*The eternal is constantly astir in everything.*

Johann Wolfgang von Goethe


*But souls that of His own good life partake,*
*He loves as His own self; dear as His eye*
*They are to Him: He'll never them forsake:*
*When they shall die, then God himself shall die;*
*They live, they live in blest eternity.*

Henry More


*Death is a necessary part of love.*
*Love and death go hand in hand and love is not complete until death takes us to the land beyond.*

Louis Richard Batzler

# Chapter 8

# Help for the Dying — A Succinct Summary

The following information is a succinct summary of ways to help the dying. This information is available in a pamphlet, *Through the Valley of the Shadow* from *The Gotach Center for Health*. Clergy, churches, hospital personnel, hospices and others who work with the dying have used this pamphlet for educational purposes as well as for specific helps during the dying process.

1. Do all you can to make patient comfortable and free from pain.

2. Be honest with the dying. Do not minimize the seriousness of the situation. The patient preconsciously knows about impending death.

3. Be present as much as possible. Do not leave the patient alone to die. Touching is comforting.

4. Converse with patient if he so desires. Don't force patient to talk. Meet him where he is.

5. Share your own thoughts and feelings about death with patient if you feel it is indicated. This includes your belief and faith in life after death.

6. Reading some good material on the subject is sometimes helpful for patient and for you.

7. Listen — to help the patient and yourself. Dying persons can be the best teachers about death.

8. Be honest with yourself and your own feelings.

9. Look and listen for symbolic language from a patient who wants understanding and support. Children especially use symbolism regarding death.

10. Genuine love is essential for real comfort.

11. Be sensitive to when you are wanted and when you are not wanted. Patient chooses the one with whom he wants to share.

12. Patient has the right to feedback and to decisions concerning his care.

13. Humor, judiciously used, is helpful.

14. Try to help patient and loved ones find meaning in the experience.

15. Be careful how you use expressions such as "God's will" in your explanations.

16. Accept the patient's denial of death if that is as far as he can go.

17. Be willing to be the recipient of patient's anger and resentment.

18. In patient's bargaining (often symbolic) be willing to talk with him about it.

19. Help patient feel free from your hold on him — or from his hold on you. Don't make him feel guilty for his dying and leaving you.

20. Recognize that there are times when the patient's needs and your needs are opposed. Do not criticize or berate him when he disagrees with you.

21. Realize that facing death brings depression and that some pathological depression may need medical assistance.

22. Viewing the body — especially after sudden death — is important for the mental health of survivors.

23. Loved ones should be assured that all that is possible is being done for patient. A follow-up several weeks after death concerning some questions that might not have been answered is often helpful.

24. The involvement of clergy in the dying process is important for emotional and spiritual support of patient and loved ones.

25. Allow patient to die his own death. If patient knows he is loved and trusted, the burden is lightened.

26. Realize that a dying person needs a genuine friend more than professional therapists.

*There is a Reaper whose name is Death,*
*And with his sickle keen,*
*He reaps the bearded grain at a breath,*
*And the flowers that grow between.*

Henry Wadsworth Longfellow


*Death is not nearer to the aged than to the new-born;*
*neither is life.*

Kahlil Gibran

# Chapter 9
# Children and Death

## I. The Well Child

Although the number of child deaths in America has decreased considerably within the last seventy-five years due to the medical progress in conquering fatal childhood diseases, many children still die from cancer, malnutrition, abuse, accidents, homicide and suicide. Death is also, very early in life, a part of children's everyday experience in the games they play, TV and films they see, books they read, and nursery rhymes they hear. Despite the pervasiveness of the death theme in children's lives, and the resultant actual or potential problems, death education for children is still not a significant part of their educational experience. Children's questions about where one comes from (birth) are being dealt with, but the question about where one is going (death) is still largely avoided. Death education today is where sex education was about twenty-five years ago. The avoiding, dismissing, evading of a child's questions and concerns about death, can increase the anxiety, trauma and denial, and sow the seeds for future death-related anxieties and psychiatric problems.[1]

Every adult has experienced or will experience a child's death and has or will have to answer a child's questions about death. It is important that adults, for their own emotional and mental health as well as that of the questioning child, be aware of facts and factors in death and dying. The problem of dealing with death concepts and experiences of children is a difficult one. For example, cultural, religious, regional, socio-economic diversity of parents and children preclude simple generalizations or easy answers. Other qualifying factors include the general developmental level or maturity, individual personality, life experiences, (especially those that are death or separation-related), and extent of communication and support from family, friends, caretakers and teachers. The complexity of the subject is further seen in the conflicting evidence that research presents in the area of death and children. However, there are some guidelines that are generally accepted as basic, and although age itself is not necessarily a primary factor, age groupings do provide a convenient framework to note specific dynamics of children's attitudes and responses to death and dying.

*Ages 3–5:* These children do not yet accept death. They often fantasize about life and death. They are still working on the idea of end and do not conceive of annihilation. They think of life, growth and death as a changing and reversible process, not final. In games they play, when one dies, he comes alive again and play is resumed. Death is sometimes seen as a sleep.

*Ages 5–9:* Children in this age grouping are beginning to understand death as end, as possibly irreversible, but they do not universalize death, nor consider it inevitable, nor think of death as happening to themselves. Though death is still remote, they begin to see it as a result of physiological processes through aging and disease. They may personify death as the "death man" or "the ghost" who is selective and carries off a few. Death is a departure.

*Ages 9 and up:* Most children begin to universalize death at this age. They are beginning to understand some of the biological aspects and believe that they too will die sometime, somewhere. These children also may view death as punishment for wrongdoing. Death is seen as inevitable, irreversible, natural and personal. There is the beginning of the integration of death-related facts and realities. The extent of this integration depends on the qualifying factors noted above.

Questions children ask about death take many forms. It is important to try to discover what is behind the question being asked. You need not always give answers, but you should recognize and respect the child's questioning. Sometimes wondering and exploring is more valuable than giving specific answers.

The questions and answers below are typical. These, and similar questions, provide a basis for discussion and for helping children and adults to become more aware and comfortable with the reality of death.

How would you answer these questions? Circle the best answer or answers. Add your own.

*What is death?* a) It's when the body stops working, the heart stops beating. b) It's a part of life. c) It's the end. d) It's when you go to heaven. e) It's the beginning of a new life. f) It's when the real you leaves your body. g) It's a change in life. h) It's not being here anymore. i) Other.

*Does everyone die?* a) Yes. b) Neither you nor I will die for a long time. c) Only sick people. d) Other.

*When will you die?* a) I don't know. b) Not for a long time. c) When I get old. d) I won't die if I keep myself healthy. e) I try to be careful so I won't have an accident. f) Probably in about thirty years. g) Other.

*Who will take care of me if you die?* a) God. b) Someone will. c) I don't know for sure. d) Your grandmother. e) You can take care of yourself. f) We have provided in our will for your Aunt _____ to raise you. g) Other.

*What happens to people after they die?* a) They go to heaven. b) They go to be with the angels. c) I don't know, but it must be good because it's with God. d) Nothing. e) We don't see them any more. f) They are buried. g) We miss them and think about them. h) They live and grow in spirit. i) Other.

*Where is he?* a) Sleeping. b) He has gone away. c) He's gone to be with God. d) He's dead. e) He's passed away. f) His body is in the ground, but his soul is with God. g) He's where he is happy. h) He's living in another world. i) Other.

*What happens to the body after they bury it?* a) It decomposes and turns to dust. b) It turns into a star. c) It stays in the ground. d) It goes to heaven. e) It rots. f) It turns into a skeleton. g) Other.

*Is there a heaven?* a) No. b) Yes. c) I don't know. d) It depends on what you mean by heaven. e) Is there love? f) Other.

*Why is she lying down in the casket?* a) So we can see her more fully. b) They want us to think of her as being comfortable, so she's lying down peacefully. c) The funeral director put her that way. d) We like to remember her as sleeping. e) Other.

*Why is he all dressed up in the casket?* a) That is probably what he was wearing when he died. b) That's his favorite outfit. c) They want us to remember him as he was before he became sick, so he is dressed up in his best clothes. d) They want him to be happy in his grave. e) Sign of respect. f) Other.

*Is she coming back?* a) No. b) Yes. c) Maybe. d) We'll see. e) She's gone to be with God. f) Her memory will stay with us. g) Other.

*What makes people die?* a) God is ready for him now. b) Sometimes accidents, disease, old age, war or violence. c) It happens to everyone sometime. d) Other.

*Did God make him die?* a) Yes. God controls everything. b) No. c) God is sad too. d) No, the disease made him die. e) No, the enemy in the war killed him. f) No, his body was too worn out to be used any more. g) Other.

*It was my fault, wasn't it?* a) You feel it was your fault? b) Sort of. If you'd played with her, she wouldn't have been in the accident. c) No, of course not. d) No. What will be, will be. e) With all the noise in the house Grandma couldn't get enough rest. f) Why do you say that? g) Other.

Analogies are often helpful in answering children's questions.

*What is death?*
A musician plays the piano and the piano seems alive. When the musician leaves, the piano is quiet.
The house is old and dilapidated. You can't live in it any more.
"I" go on living. My "body" goes back to the ground.
The clothes are worn out. He can't wear them any more. His body is like his clothes.
There are cycles of life — buds mature, wither, and fall. New buds come on the same tree. Summer is life. Winter is death-like.

*What happens to people when they die?*
We play a record, learn a song, and sing it, even after the record breaks. The song lives on. What will the new life be like? A baby in the womb can't imagine the next world.
It's like the caterpillar who changes into a butterfly.

*What causes death?*
Old age: The body is worn out. The house is dilapidated.
Accidents: A rosebud is accidently snipped off. A baby bird falls out of the nest. A tree is blown over in the wind.
Disease: We do not know all we need to know to keep ourselves healthy.
War and violence: There are many causes.

Death is not to be a "hush-hush" subject with children. The commonly used euphemistic phrases such as "he passed away," "the departed one," "she's gone to sleep" can be more harmful than helpful.

In addition to answering specific questions, there are many ways that adults can informally and effectively educate children about death and offer comfort.

These include:

1. Offer children early opportunities for casual conversation: when driving past a cemetery, when reading appropriate newspaper items, or watching television.

2. Discuss experiences of death in birds, flowers, fish, animals, pets, seasonal changes.

3. Involve children in the experience when acquaintances or friends of the family meet death as well as when close relatives and immediate family members die. Children can be taken to the funeral home, to the funeral and to visit the bereaved family. When children attend a funeral home or funeral, you should be careful to comfort, touch and answer their questions so that their fears or anxieties are avoided or minimized. The seeds for various phobias can be planted during the funeral experience if the child's questions or concerns are not dealt with.

One middle-aged woman who had claustrophobia and agoraphobia was hypnotically regressed to her childhood and in that space she recalled that she had fearfully watched the lid of the casket being closed over her dead grandfather and the casket put in the ground. In subsequent analysis by the therapist, it was revealed that this episode was a major cause of her phobias.

Children are not to be forced to attend funeral

homes or funerals nor should they be forced to do things against their will at the funeral home.

One nurse working on a psychiatric unit related the story of a young boy who was forced by his parent to kiss his dead uncle on the cheek as he lay in the casket. Several weeks later the boy was admitted needing psychiatric help. Treatment revealed that his problem originated from the forced act of kissing the dead person.

Involve children in family rituals, visiting the cemetery, contributing to a memorial or special fund, creating a gift or drawing for the bereaved. Respect their ideas of showing love, grief and concern at the time of death or at anniversaries.

A unique example of this is the case of two young boys, one of whose grandfather died. They built a tree hut which represented heaven. One boy played God and lowered dolls to the other. This represented birth. The other boy on the ground tied a doll to the string which was pulled up to heaven. This represented death.

4. Be aware of possible guilt feelings a child may have over the death of a loved one and deal with this guilt as quickly as possible. Children sometimes feel responsible for the death of a loved one, especially if they've "wished" the deceased one dead in a moment of anger. This often happens in the case of sibling death. Children also see death as punishment which causes guilt and fear.

5. Be aware of the child's fear of being deserted when a loved one dies. Reassurance needs to be given to the child that he will not be deserted. Anger, frustration and resentment can easily emerge from this unresolved fear. Do not physically or emotionally isolate the child.

A seven-year-old child whose father died expressed this fear of desertion by having to sleep with his mother every night thereafter and frequently had choking spells when his mother was not near him. He claimed that he choked so that his mother would come to him and thereby he could see that she had not deserted him.

6. A surviving child reacts to the loss of a sibling and to the changed behavior of his parents and others. Parents need to reassure the siblings that the depth of their grief does not negate the love for the siblings.

7. Welcome the child's discussing the death and be sensitive to his feelings. Even though a child's grief is usually resolved quicker than an adult's grief, one session is hardly enough. There needs to be an on-going working out of the grief. Surviving siblings had a close relationship with the dead sibling. Grief will exaggerate positive and negative feelings between the children. The death of a sibling may also cause the surviving children to fear that their own death is imminent.

8. Be sensitive to the child's fears of doctors and hospitals, when these have been related to the death of a loved one. Also, be sensitive to a child's fear of death when he gets sick.

9. Do not be afraid to show emotion before children. Silence from parents can be difficult to cope with.

10. Listen to your child's silence. A child's silence does not mean there are no feelings or questions. Look for ways to have him "open up." One mother found her grieving son, who had lost his

brother, talking and crying openly after many months of silence as they rode home together one night after church. The mother felt this opening came from the church service plus the darkness which masked face-to-face encounter.

11. Realize that children find it easier to "mourn at a distance" or vicariously, such as showing great empathy for characters in a book, play or film, but little apparent grief for the deceased. Also, the child may overreact to trivia such as a broken toy or a lost coin.

12. Be aware that a child may assume mannerisms or symptoms of the deceased, or, in the case of a sibling, wear the deceased's clothes or play with his toys.

13. Continue to answer questions about the deceased even long after the death. Each new stage of growth elicits new questions.

14. Be honest, explaining truthfully to children on a level they can understand. Try to realize where a child is in his total life period when discussing death. To know where a child is coming from helps you to know where to lead him. Answer all questions simply and directly. Do not give him information that will need to be unlearned. Do not tell him fantasies in his grief. Be careful how you talk about God and the death event.

## II. The Dying Child

The dying child presents one of the most tragic and traumatic challenges to parents and health professionals. Today, through much clinical research, new understandings and treatments of the dying child are being discovered and carried out. These advances are helping not only the patient, but also the parents and caretakers to better cope.

What the well child might only faintly glimpse about death and dying, the dying child now experiences in stark reality. Generally, the dying child "grows up" quickly and achieves a maturity in some aspects of his life even beyond that of his parents. The dying child eventually comes to know preconsciously that he is dying.[2] This awareness is reinforced by the acquisition of information from many sources — friends, parents, doctors, nurses, other patients, body changes, hushed conversations, new procedures or movement to other locations, etc. This does not mean that the child will speak freely about his dying, even with ones he trusts.[3] Many of his coping strategies are denial-based. Communication often comes from the dying child symbolically through drawings, body language and particular foci of attention.

A child's awareness of his dying raises the question — as it does with dying adults also — of the caretakers' and parents' responsibility in disclosing that information to the patient. Adult silence may cause the child not to express his death awareness and fears, but when given the opportunity, he usually will, and, as a result, feels less lonely and isolated.[4] Results of a survey of 97 pediatricians concerning attitudes and practices of "telling" children reveal that the majority felt that dying children should be informed of the diagnosis only when they ask, and should not be informed of their prognosis. One out of five respondents said parents should usually be told of their dying child's diagnosis and 64 percent of those in practice under 10 years felt parents should be given accurate prognosis on request.[5]

Two of the main fears of the dying child are pain and separation. For the normal, well child, these are traumatic; for the dying, they are especially so. If the child adds to these fears the fact that death is coming as a punishment, the pain can increase and separation can become serration of the psyche. Recognition of these factors emphasizes the need for dying children to know that they have been loved, are loved, and will be loved no matter what they have been or done. There is no substitute for the presence of loving parents and caretakers for the dying child.

Just as the normal, well child's approach to death is qualified by a number of factors, so is the dying child's approach — although with the dying child the factors are now experiential. The attitudes and behavior of a dying child are greatly determined by the way he is able to integrate and synthesize information. This is more apparent in the older child.

In the very young dying child (3 to 5 years), you may see strange behavior, almost appearing to be psychotic, such as hallucinations, delusions, fantasies, obvious distorted reality. Such behavior is not psychotic, but is the response of a tender body, mind and spirit to severe stress. A child this age does not have mature ego defenses to cope with the stresses and thus uses primitive coping mechanisms. Unlike the mature adult who is dying and who often goes through recognizable stages, the little child's behavior takes many unanticipated shifts. It is important for parents and caretakers to realize this and strive to be understanding and patient. It is also important for parents and caretakers to be present as much as possible, touching and having much interaction and coordination of efforts.

From 6 to 12 years, there is usually more in-touch-ness with one's death. This child more readily assimilates and integrates the accumulated information. As the dying process moves on, the child's self-image changes and his attitudes and behavior become more defined.[6] The adolescent patient does not dwell on death and is not likely to freely share what he knows. He may exhibit a concern about wasting time, avoid conversation about goals or the future, express anxiety about debilitation and insist that things be done right away. The focus is on everyday activities. This should also be the focus of the family and caretakers. Avoiding attention to the disease, fostering of family and peer relationships, normalizing daily living and continually reassuring the child that you will return are ways of facilitating this focus.

The dying teen-ager faces death the way he faces life — in contradictory and perplexing ways. Therefore, you can expect a great variety of responses in his dying. This is the stage in which the person is searching for meaning, purpose, goals, values, fulfillment in life — graduation, vocation, courtship, marriage, identity and independence. The awareness of impending death often intensifies this search and this, in turn, intensifies denial, anger, frustration and repressive mechanisms. Frank depression may be apparent, but suicidal inclinations are relatively rare in the dying teen-ager. This is an interesting contrast to the well teen-ager who statistically has the highest incidence of suicide.

There is an increased importance of the body image so the special meaning of disability, disfigurement and death must be realized and dealt with. Many dying teen-agers evince a compassion for their parents and develop ways to protect or comfort the parents.

The dying teen-ager can be helped through humor, continuity of care, identifying and involving a "hero" for the patient, affirming and confirming his identity, establishing trust through honesty and clarity, normalization of his life and including the patient in decisions concerning treatment.

In caring for the dying child, medical personnel often experience a pattern of anticipatory grief similar to the family members. To avoid this personal trauma, caretakers focus on the physical and diagnostic aspects of the case. Avoidance is a common behavior of caretakers. This is not helpful to patient or family and creates other stresses (guilt, frustration, anger) which cause problems specifically affecting patient care such as carelessness or forgetfulness. This particular problem of caretakers points up the importance of total or holistic care, involving the entire health care team.[7]

There are many specific ways in which doctors and nurses can help the dying children and their parents.

1. Prepare parents and patient for what they will experience (machines, tubes, treatment, etc.) beforehand.

2. Allow parents to be present during treatment and let them be involved in their child's care as much as possible.

3. Anticipate questions, give simple answers and don't "talk down" to families.

4. Be honest. Tell what you know and also what you don't know about the child's condition.

5. Be willing to express your emotions (sadness, frustrations, anger) and give parents "permission" to express theirs.

6. Be patient in repeating information for parents. Their denial and grief preclude their hearing and absorbing clearly.

7. Reassure parents and child that everything possible is being done and that you will not give up on the case.

8. Arrange for the parents to be with the child at the moment of death. Allow them as much time as they need alone with the child after death.

9. Answer parents' questions especially about the child's pain and fear.

10. Relate to both parents equally when giving information.

11. Be gentle and kind in caring for the child.

12. Do whatever you can for the parents after the child dies. Don't rush away. Refer to the child by name.

13. The comforting touch for parents is very important.

14. Attend the funeral if you are genuinely inclined to do so.

15. Ask parents about organ donations and reas-

sure them that their child's body will be treated with respect and dignity.

*And I think that there isn't a doctor who doesn't want to be more than a doctor, even if they feel that they were called to the profession. And there isn't a doctor who doesn't feel bereft when they have to deal with telling somebody that somebody has died or that they are going to die. They don't quite know what to do with it. They're caught in denial and they don't want to be caught in denial. To treat the human being and to have to look away from their eyes. That hurts, as fellow human beings. I think the medical community would like to be more comfortable in the human roles in the world.*

Ram Dass

*When you pass through the waters, I will be with you; and when you pass through the rivers, they will not sweep over you. When you walk through the fire, you will not be burned.*

Isaiah 43:2

*To take something that happens to every human being and make it into a failure is immediately the creation of suffering for everyone.*

Ram Dass

# Chapter 10
# Death and the Physician

The physician has a key role in the life of every patient. In the case of the dying patient, the physician becomes involved in some special dynamics and dimensions which cannot be regarded lightly. The way a patient and the family cope with the dying process is frequently determined by the attitude and care of the attending physician(s). Although cure (doing to) is the major motivation and goal of the physician, care (doing with) cannot be neglected.

The impending and actual death of a patient may magnify feelings of impotence, ineptness, failure or even guilt in the physician. Much of the literature on attitudes and behavior of medical practitioners notes that they associate dying patients with personal failure and tend to avoid them or spend as little time as possible with them. In one sample of 73 medical doctors, only 13 consented to an interview regarding dying patients. The others refused when told what the subject of the interview was.[1]

> The fact that death is seen as an enemy creates a sense of failure in the practitioner every time somebody dies because the practitioner gets attached. You do your healing because that's the part you play. You're a healer. But you don't identify with being a healer, you identify with being somebody who is working on yourself and somebody who is playing a part. Whether the healing works is in God's hands,

not in your hands. A philosophic materialist patient gets very eager to put trust in the Doctor, the Doctor gets caught in playing God and feeling like he is responsible — but God is responsible. So, what happens is, because of the pain, the practitioners feel when a patient dies — and they've put all kinds of juice into it — the attachment to the goal makes the pain so great for most Doctors that they close their heart. They become professionally warm, but they don't allow their hearts to stay open.[2]

It is important that physicians, for their own mental and emotional health as well as that of the dying patient and family, be sensitive and responsive to the various particular needs of the patient. The following are guidelines to help the physician with this concern.

1. See the dying patient as a person of unique worth and be honest, clear and open with the patient and family. There is conflicting information concerning the attitudes and practice of physicians in this matter. One survey of 151 physicians in 10 medical specialties led the authors to conclude that most physicians feel that the patient should be told about terminal illness regardless of physical status, age and life expectancy.[3] Another study of 219 physicians' policies about truth-telling showed that 90 percent of the sample indicated a preference for not telling cancer patients the truth about their illness.[4] Many nurses who attended the *Gotach Center for Health* seminars on Death and Dying reported that more physicians preferred not to tell the "whole story" or did so reluctantly. Research and experience reveal that the majority of patients wish to be told of their terminal condition and usually suffer little or no

long-term negative consequences as a result of being informed.[5] To deny the patient information is to deprive him of the choice to live out his days meaningfully or even to deprive him of the opportunity to fight for life.

> I cannot conceive of the practice of medicine in which there is any breach of absolute trust and confidence between patient and doctor. A good physician cannot lie to his patient. If the truth be bitter, he must help the patient face it. On the other hand, I could not bear to practice medicine if I felt obliged always to tell everything I know or think I know. In a materialistic age, in a society which is certainly notable for individual bravery, independence of thought, or a philosophic attitude, it will not be possible to make a philosopher out of every man during the terminal illness. Perhaps Sir William Jenner's three essential qualities for the medical man will see us through such difficult times; "He must be honest, he must be dogmatic, he must be kind."[6]

2. Be aware and sensitive to the mental, emotional and spiritual pains of the patient and give some attention to these as well as to the patient's physical pain. In effect, to help facilitate safe conduct through the valley of the shadow. Sometimes physicians tend to label dying patients as "good" or "troublesome" and treat them accordingly. One nurse described a surgeon who, when he discovered in surgery that his patients' conditions were inoperable, sewed them up and had no more communication with them afterward.

3. Include patient and family in decisions regarding the patient's illness and treatment.

4. Do not set deadlines or dates for a patient's death. Some patients are devastated when this categorical type of information is given to them.

Diagnosis can usually be ascertained; prognosis is less certain. Information can be phrased positively. The patient can be informed of his reasonable minimal life expectancy rather than of the probable date of his death. Also, the physician may indicate his professional opinion is not infallible.

5. Recognize the value of and include other support persons and groups in working with the patient, e.g., clergy, social workers, psychologists, hospice personnel. Be open and willing to meet with or consult other professional staff persons (physicians, nurses, therapists, chaplains) to discuss the case.

This team approach is especially important in those difficult situations involving life support systems that prolong life. The physician should respect the patient's religion, philosophy and wishes concerning the way he chooses to die. Each situation needs to be assessed individually because of the many variables.

In the so-called "hopeless case," the physician might well consider the following:

a. The physician is fallible and the case may *not* be medically "hopeless."
b. The physician by tradition has been committed to *active* contention with disease.
c. The physician is not competent to determine fully the "quality" of a given life or whether longevity is "fruitless."
d. Even if without positive act, the physician who arrogates to himself the prerogative of determining whether life shall continue or terminate by default is in an uncomfortable moral position.
e. The discovery of new curative agents is an ever-present possibility.

f. Spontaneous regression of malignancies in apparently "hopeless" patients has been documented.

g. Miraculous intervention is possible.

h. The physician may find that self-recrimination at errors of omission is harsher than at errors of commission.

i. Even a brief moment of mental lucidity in a moribund patient may be all-important for his spiritual welfare.

j. "Extraordinary" means of treatment may result in cure.[7]

## 6. Get in touch with one's own thoughts and feelings about death and work on that.

And, a doctor who thinks he can come off the freeway, jump out of his car, walk in and do it, is missing the point of the game. The doctor's own fear of his own death is creating additional fear in the patient. He's going in with penicillan and drugs, but at the same moment he's also going in with his own fear of death. . . . Well the doctor is conveying the same fear of death and that fear is making the healing process harder. So that they are going against even what they are trying to do by their unwillingness to examine the issue of death and seeing death as just an enemy that you push away at all costs. So, the doctors' unwillingness to work on themselves is one of the most contraproductive aspects of their training and their work as healer.[8]

## 7. Provide opportunity for the family to ventilate when death occurs by explaining, sympathizing, reassuring that everything was done for the patient.

The many responsibilities and challenges that physicians have in their daily work, combined with the main purpose of their vocation — to cure — and their individual difficulties in dealing with the dying, mean that frequently physicians will overlook or by-pass some of the above guidelines.

There are ways to help the physician.

1. Patients and family members can help physicians by being direct, honest and clear about their desires, expectations and information that they want to know. Writing out specific questions and concerns is helpful. Direct and firm confrontation with the physician is sometimes necessary. Such comments to the physician as, "Whose life is it?" or "Who is paying you?" can often bring results.

2. Nurses can be facilitators of good communication and relationships between patient, family and physician by providing the physician with information about patient concerns and needs, and helping families understand medical terminology, hospital policies and procedures. Sometimes nurses confront the physician and, though risky, thereby help all concerned.

3. Physicians need comfort and support in their work with the dying — especially with dying children. Suggesting or providing counsel, formal or informal, can be a welcome aid to anguishing doctors. Caring for the doctor is also caring for the patient and family.

4. Advocating and helping to implement interdisciplinary staff meetings can be valuable for all who are working with the dying.

5. Increased death education for students in medical schools and for practicing physicians. Various surveys of death education in U.S. medical schools indicate that few full-term courses are offered. A 1973 report of 83 medical schools, showed 42 had no formal program on the dying

patient, 12 indicated the subject was dealt with informally and 8 planned a course.[9] A 1975 survey of 107 medical schools revealed 7 with full-term courses on death, 44 had a "minicourse" and 42 a lecture or two. Seventy-one percent of the schools reporting require that at least half of their students be exposed to some death education.[10]

In summary, the physician is to be a friend who is aware of the road that lies ahead and is willing to go along that road with the patient no matter how torturous, trusting that the human spirit is too sacred and precious for the death of the body to be its final event.

The physician is much more than a mechanic whose business is to prolong life. He is a fellow pilgrim on the journey of life and needs to be willing to be sensitively present in the patient's perilous passage.

*Let not your heart be troubled: ye believe in God,
believe also in me.*

*In my Father's house are many mansions: if it were
not so, I would have told you, I go to prepare a place
for you.*

*And if I go and prepare a place for you, I will come
again, and receive you unto myself; that where I am,
there ye may be also. . . .*

*I will not leave you comfortless: I will come to you. . . .*

*Peace I leave with you, my peace I give unto you:
not as the world giveth, give I unto you. Let not your
heart be troubled, neither let it be afraid.*

Jesus the Christ


*Now our wants and burdens leaving
To His care who cares for all,
Cease we fearing, cease we grieving,
At His touch our burdens fall.*

Samuel Longfellow


*Be Thou, O Rock of Ages, nigh!
So shall each murmuring thought be gone;
And grief and fear and care shall fly,
As clouds before the mid-day sun.*

Charles Wesley


*Be not afraid of those trials which God may see fit to
send upon thee. It is with the wind and storm of tribula-
tion that God separates the true wheat from the chaff.
Always remember, therefore, that God comes to thee in
thy sorrows, as really as in thy joys. He lays low, and
He builds up. Thou wilt find thyself far from perfection,
if thou dost not find God in everything.*

Miguel de Molinos

# Chapter 11
# Grief

A basic factor in the understanding of grief is that all relationships eventually end in separation. The nature of the relationship largely determines the nature of the grief. The loss of a casual acquaintance, where there is some mutuality and risk, usually does not elicit the intensity of grief that the loss of a good friend does. With the loss of a friend, the benevolent forces of trust, responsibility, openness and sharing are lost and these losses can shatter your inner security system. When the loss is that of a deeply loved one, where there has been intimacy, risk, vulnerability, trust, sharing and mutual delight in one's presence, then grief is usually extreme. Here separation is serration. No one fully recovers from the loss of a significant loved one. The mature adult is really a mourning person. We part at many levels and when this happens a rich process of grieving is set off.

From shortly after birth until a person dies, grief is a significant part of one's life. There are many reasons for grief, and grief has many manifestations, ramifications, intensities, and durations. The increased awareness and understanding of the complexity and significance of grief have resulted in much responsible and valuable research and therapy for the prevention and healing of grief-related distresses.

Basically, grief is that difficult and painful constellation of thoughts and feelings that you experience through separation, loss or significant change. Grief is a universal experience and, as such, it is important to realize that grief is not a sign of weakness, nor lack of faith, but a human need. Grief is an expression of love that is honorable, cathartic and therapeutic. Grief teaches. Through grief you can see priorities and perspectives more clearly and experience deep feelings more intensely. This seeing and feeling are helpful for growth toward wholeness. Grief can also establish and strengthen relationships which become supportive and help to fill the vacuum of loneliness. It is important, therefore, to begin grief "work" as soon as possible. Postponed, suspended or unresolved grief can be detrimental to your physical, mental, emotional and spiritual health. The loss of a loved one is not easy. It is even more difficult when you do not deal with the loss. If you do not deal with the loss, you run the risk of losing yourself.

> An interesting example of unresolved grief is that of a sixty-five year old bachelor whose mother died when he was ten. His grief was expressed in anger and resentment for her deserting him. As he grew older, he transferred this unresolved anger and resentment to women in general and, as a result, precluded meaningful relations with women.

Grief can bring about a number of changes in your body, mind and spirit. Physically, practically all of the bodily systems can be affected. The muscular system might develop weakness, paralysis, tremors, fatigue, tension. The glandular systems — tear, salivary, sexual — are usually affected and the cardiovascular system can react through blood pressure changes, rapid and irregular heartbeat, body temperature changes, asthma, respiration changes and headache. Resistance to infection is often reduced so that various types of diseases might emerge. The gastrointestinal system reacts through nausea, swelling, loss of appetite, indigestion, bowel dysfunction.

Grief also involves the mind, emotions and spirit. Many of these expressions of grief are noted below. There is no right or wrong way to grieve. It is wrong, however, to impose your own way of grieving on others. A tragic example of this is that of a wife whose husband died suddenly. She did not cry and demanded that her two children not cry and did not allow them to attend the funeral of their father. A few weeks later the teen-age son was in a mental institution.

As each person lives uniquely, so each grieves uniquely. Thus the times, stages, variety and intensity of one's grief will vary. The following information is not a construction of how to grieve, but guidelines to help persons be sensitive to significant and specific dynamics and dimensions of grief.

## Time Frame

One week, several weeks or months.

## Characteristics

Cognitive confusion. One has not yet comprehended full significance of loss. Experience is like a bad dream. Feelings of numbness, trance-likeness, blunting of feelings, yet sensitive to hurts.

## Special Needs

Support from loves ones, but not over-support. A need for emotional distance and some solitude and privacy.

Grieving families report that one of the most helpful and meaningful experiences for them is the presence of nurses at funerals, or receiving some form of condolence from those who have cared for their loved ones during their illness.

## Tasks

To maintain integrity of self; not to fall apart. Carrying out day-to-day functions.

## Time Frame

Many months.

## Characteristics

Usually this is the most difficult time. Shock has diminished. People are not around as before. May experience aimlessness, depression, loneliness, frenzied activity, apathy, fatigue, loss of appetite, sleeplessness, poor memory, frequent weeping, feelings of craziness, self-pity, anger, guilt, resentment, fear, desire to be punished, death-wish, hostility to God, loss of faith, hope, love, sense of loss of selfhood and meaning. These latter emotions have their positive counterparts, e.g., renewal of faith, hope, love, goals, intentions and purposes which enhance selfhood. Person may also experience hallucinations or presence of loved one through voice, vision or dreams of the deceased. Some desire to contact the deceased through seance. Sometimes there is a radical change in life style.

One mother, whose young daughter died, dreamed of her each night walking with other children in a circle, all holding lighted candles. Her daughter's candle, however, was not lit and when the mother, in the dream, asked her daughter why her candle was not lit, the little girl answered that it was because the mother's tears had put it out. The mother sought help for her grief and the dream ceased.

One dying person, during her denial stage (which is one expression of anticipatory grief) dreamed of a kindly robed figure who walked past her, but she could not see his face. Months later, after accepting her dying, she had the same dream, but this time saw the face of the figure. It was that of Christ.

Another example of how a dream helped persons in their grief is the case of a sister and mother who were in deep grief over the sudden accidental death of the brother/son. Neither had seen the body which heightened the grief. One night the man came to his sister in a dream, appearing whole and assuring her he was all right. That same night he appeared in a dream to his mother also. When sister and mother shared their same dream, they were both greatly relieved. The synchronicity of these dreams suggests the possibility of a visitation of the man's spirit rather than a formal dream.

Precognitive dreams, voices and visions frequently happen concerning deaths. One case involved a pregnant woman whose deceased grandmother appeared in a dream telling her that her baby would be born dead. Several days later the stillbirth occurred.

A nurse reported her 12-year-old daughter heard Jesus say to her that he was coming to take her with him. A week later the child died.

Another mother said that her 2-year-old daughter told her father several times that God had said to her that she would die before she was 3 years old. The last message came on a Friday. On Sunday, while blowing up a balloon at a birthday party, the child sucked the balloon into her windpipe and choked to death.

## Special Needs

Desire to talk about deceased and details of death. There is a need for reassurance that all was done to help the one who died. Important to have support groups and individuals. Begin to normalize life again.

### Tasks

Admit and accept the pain and reality of the loss. Be willing to talk out thoughts, feelings, memories with caring persons. See the experience in the perspective of one's past, present and future. Renew relationships.

## Time Frame

Several weeks, months or years. Two or more years possible in the case of suicide, murder or sudden death. Also, long periods of grief may be experienced in a child's death and elderly who lose a spouse.

## Characteristics

Greater sense of peace and stability. Regaining a sense of a fruitful and hopeful future. Painful memories may crop up occasionally. Mourning process reaching completion.

## Special Needs

Putting "one's house in order" (financial, legal, etc.). Normalization proceeding.

## Tasks

Seeking work or activities to give life meaning. Restoring ego integrity. Recognizing the value of faith.

Sudden and accidental death, suicide and murder often set off grief reactions that need professional attention. However, there are special support measures by caretakers that can be offered immediately to help the suddenly bereaved.

1. Ideally, the physician should be the one to inform the family of the death.

2. Families should be allowed, even encouraged, to see the body as soon as possible after death. If there is severe mutilation, some effort should be made to let the family see a part of the body or touch the covered body. This facilitates the grief process and helps to confirm the reality of the death which is so important in grief resolution.

> One mother reported how, in the last days of her daughter's death from a contagious disease, she was not allowed to see her daughter even after she died. Several years later, this mother was still in deep grief.

3. Intense feelings by family or attending caretakers should not be subdued. The bereaved appreciate genuine sharing in their grief by caretakers.

4. Communication with the family during the dying and immediately after the death and later is most helpful. Be truthful.

5. Reassure the family that everything possible is being done or was done to save the patient.

6. When possible, arrange for family members to be with the patient at the moment of death, if they want to be there. Allow them as much time as they need to be with the deceased.

7. Refer to the patient by name, especially after death.

8. After breaking the sad news, don't rush away. Involve other comforters. Touching the bereaved is important.

9. Be discerning in offering medication for the bereaved.

10. Accept the bereaved's denial which is an emotional protection in the traumatic situation.

11. Don't give rationalizations about the patient's death, e.g., that he would have been a burden or would have suffered if he had lived.

For the survivors who experience sudden death of a loved one, the following are suggested:

1. Realize that sudden or violent death usually takes longer to accept and work through the grief.

2. Shock and numbness are the major emotions at the time of death. The more difficult time comes later.

3. Be honest about your feelings and not ashamed to grieve openly.

4. Share your thoughts and feelings with those who have had similar experiences. Their sympathy and understanding is genuine.

5. Be willing to seek special help.

6. In your mourning, reach out to others who are also hurting.

7. Have faith in God even though you can't understand the tragedy.

One of the most difficult grief experiences is the death of a child. It is natural for a child to experience the death of a parent. A child's death reverses the natural order and makes the grief heavier. Parents who have lost children generally agree on the following:

1. Intense grieving, with ebbs and flows, may last as long as two years or more.

2. Bizarre types of behavior (such as aching arms or phantom crying which may occur in stillbirth) can be part of normal grief.

> One grieving mother, who lost her child at birth and needed psychiatric help, was instructed to visualize Jesus handing her dead baby to her. She was to sit in a rocking chair and rock while imagining her holding the baby in her arms. After several rockings each day, she was to visualize her handing the baby back to Jesus. After several days of this procedure, she was to visualize her giving the baby to Jesus and see him taking the baby and leaving in the light. This "healing of the memories" technique was successful for her.

Many hospitals today are helping parents of stillborn or newborn deaths by offering parents the opportunity to hold the dead child for awhile, taking pictures of the child, suggesting the child be given a name, helping with funeral arrangements and providing some on-the-spot counseling. If a stillborn child is deformed and the parents are informed of this, it is important that they see the baby, or some part of it. Otherwise, they may have serious problems as they imagine, for years to come, all sorts of monstrosities as their child.

3. Put off major decisions for a while until feelings have stabilized.

4. Allow sufficient time to mourn and recover emotional and physical strength.

5. If you have another pregnancy, choose a new name for the child.

6. The special "bonding" between mother and child (which begins before birth) means a mother's grief will probably be longer and more intense. But the father's and sibling's grief is intense also. Twins also have a special "bonding" which often affects their grieving.

7. The anniversary of a child's death can be especially stressful. Allow emotional space and time for grieving.

> One nurse reported that her 9-year-old son drowned while her 6-year-old son watched. Her 6-year-old son is now 9 and, as he remembers his brother's death, he is having fears about his dying now at this age. This child is receiving professional help. This same fear can be seen in adults who remember a parent or sibling dying at a certain age and then, as they approach that age, begin to take on similar symptoms that the dying parent or sibling had and talk about dying at about the same age. This type of fear often needs therapeutic intervention.

8. Be patient and loving toward the surviving siblings who may exhibit unpleasant behavior such as bedwetting, impaired learning, aggressive activity.

9. Share belongings of your dead child with siblings or special friends.

Bereaved parents suggest the following ways for family and friends to help them in their grieving process.

1. Be available, get in touch, encourage others to visit or help.

2. Share your sorrow and allow parents to express their grief.

3. Be a good listener, but also accept silence and do not force conversation, especially trivia.

4. Don't tell parents what they should feel or do; also encourage them to be patient with themselves and not to impose "shoulds" on themselves.

5. Be willing to talk about endearing qualities of the child they have lost. Parents do not know all of the qualities of their children and appreciate what others can tell them.

6. Be mindful and supportive of the grieving brothers and sisters. They are sometimes neglected and need special attention. They may feel responsible for the death of the sibling. Give them opportunities for expressing their grief, such as drawing, writing, sports.[1]

7. Don't try to find something positive in the child's death, or don't say that they have other children or that they can have another child.

8. Reassure parents that all was done medically to save the child from death, if you know this is true.

9. Realize that both parents are in deep grief and

not likely to be able to support one another. Thus, the strength and support of close friends and relatives are most important. There is an exceptionally high divorce rate among parents who lose children early. Professional intervention is often needed to prevent this.

Bereaved parents often look to doctors and nurses for comfort in their grief. These caretakers can help.

1. Reassure families that everything possible was done for their child.

2. Honestly answer parents' questions about the pain and fear their child experienced.

3. Comfort *both* parents in their grief and help them take the next steps in their shock and confusion.

4. If possible, visit funeral home and/or attend the funeral.

5. Be sensitive to physical and emotional distresses of the parents, but don't over-medicate.

The following includes, in abbreviated form, comments concerning grief and bereavement. This information is available in quantity in a pamphlet, *Beside Still Waters* from the *Gotach Center for Health* and can be used in family, parish, hospice, and hospital work.

## GENERAL OBSERVATIONS

The grief process may begin at the time of awareness of death's being near as well as during and after the death event.

Grief is more complex than we usually realize.

Grief is a therapeutic experience.

Persons have resources within them to handle grief.

Grief often brings distorted behavior patterns.

Grief needs to be worked through and the sooner the better — especially in sudden death.

Most often the greatest grief is from the loss of a spouse.

## POSSIBLE TYPES OF BEHAVIOR

Withdrawal — no social responsibility.

Isolation — even from immediate family.

Hyper-irritability.

Hostility toward God, self, others.

Death wish.

Out of character behavior — e.g., hyperenergetic.

Psychosomatic illnesses — especially colitis, arthritis, asthma.

Assumes symptoms of dying person.

Depression.

Desire to be punished.

Guilt.

Fear.

Loneliness.

Tearfulness.

Bewilderment.

## HELPING ONE THROUGH GRIEF

Listen. Let person talk it out.

Realize bad feelings (e.g., guilt) need resolving, although not necessarily immediately.

Accept person's thoughts and feelings about his memories.

Be aware that the length of grief period varies with different individuals.

Assist in getting medical treatment when indicated.

Be honest with person and yourself.

Share your own grief thoughts and feelings if pertinent.

Help person become involved in other activities — at his own pace.

Be willing to be recipient of person's anger and frustration.

Be available but do not impose on person's privacy. Be sensitive to when you are wanted and when you are not wanted.

Help person to look for meaning in the experience — especially in light of his faith.

Encourage an attitude of gratitude. This may come in later reflections.

Humor, judiciously used, is helpful.

Let your love be genuine.

Affirm person's strengths, that he is O.K. and will recover.

Share in prayer.

Consider discussing person's dreams as a means of revelation and release.

Be willing to involve other caring persons to help you in your grief work.

Be aware that the body has its own wisdom and that physical movement and exercise are often excellent healers of grief.

*The only true death, the only good death, is a culminating outburst of life: it is the fruit of a desperate effort made by the living to become more pure, more stripped and bare, more taut as they force their way out of the zone in which they are imprisoned.*

Pierre Teilhard de Chardin

*He brought light out of darkness, not out of a lesser light; he can bring thy summer out of winter, though thou have no spring; though in the ways of fortune or understanding or conscience, thou have been benighted till now, wintered and frozen, clouded and eclipsed, damped and benumbed, smothered and stupified till now, now God comes to thee, not as in the dawning of the day, not as in the bud of the spring, but as the sun at noon.*

John Donne

*All human beings deserve to die with dignity and with love around them.*

Mother Teresa

# Chapter 12
# Hospice

The hospice movement in America is one of the most important resources for the dying and their loved ones. Hospices in the middle ages were places, established and managed by religious orders, which cared for the sick and wounded and offered a refuge for weary travelers. Today the hospice concept refers to a place and community of persons devoted to care for the dying and their families. Hospices of one kind or another now number more than 400 in America in virtually every state.

Hospice is an expression of care and caring for the dying, a sensitive and serious response to persons in that phase of life which too often is neglected. The hospice philosophy honors the dying and seeks to add life to the days rather than more days to life. The major thrust is care rather than cure, a concern for the whole person rather than treating an illness.

Hospice seeks to facilitate integration of the dying experience into the life cycle. The integrating process is three dimensional — an intrapersonal dimension where care is extended to support and enable acceptance and peaceful integration of impending death; an interpersonal dimension for enabling the development and continuance of human relationships between the dying and their loved ones; and a faith dimension in which the program assists each person in the search for his ultimate meaning and relationship to God. The hospice experience does not consider death in the win/lose context of medical science, but rather in the context of loss which leads to a greater life again. The task of all hospice personnel is to make dying as comfortable and as meaningful as possible by maximizing the quality of life.

Specifically, hospices

1. Help the dying to regain, if necessary, and to maintain their identity, dignity, independence, and control.

2. Assist the dying to face death without fear, anxiety, and pain.

3. Involve the family as a major caretaker and support group.

4. Facilitate an integrated dying by meeting the physical, mental, emotional, social, and spiritual needs of the dying and their families.

5. Offer support in the grief process and bereavement.

6. Utilize multidisciplinary teams to deal with the multiplicity of problems in the dying interval.

Usually these goals determine the broad outline of the hospice program. Most hospice programs include home care (at present the most prevalent), in-patient care mostly for short stays, bereavement follow-up and various educational activities for volunteers, patients and the community at large.

There are five types of hospices in America.

1. Free-standing which has its own administrative staff and place.

2. Extended care in a facility, usually a nursing home.

3. Home care (hospital without walls), which is autonomous and has twenty-four hours a day availability.

4. Hospital-affiliated, free-standing in the community, hospital owned.

5. Hospital-based, usually for short-term acute care and consultant programs.

Volunteers play a key role in hospice. They are persons who choose to be involved and to minister. The volunteers' tasks are many, e.g., clerical duties, housekeeping, staff support, patient family contacts, bereavement follow-up. What makes the volunteers valuable is not so much what they do as why they do it. It is the compassion and love that the volunteer brings that is so important. In the final analysis, this is what the dying need and desire most — a loving, caring person. Patients, families, and hospice workers all affirm that their lives have been enriched because of the love and care that is shared.

*By pitting life against death, by forcing apart and attaching self to one of them, we reduce life to the measure of our own impotence. We reject the rhythm of Creation, the condition of its renewal.*

H. L. Fausset

*We speak of reverence for life, but what about reverence for the process of dying.*

Anonymous

*It is impossible that anything so natural, so necessary and so universal as death should ever have been designed as an evil to mankind.*

Anonymous

*No longer forward nor behind*
*I look in hope or fear;*
*But, grateful, take the good I find*
*The best of now and here.*

John Greenleaf Whittier

*Living is not good, but living well. The wise man, therefore, lives as well as he should, not as long as he can. . . . He will always think of life in terms of quality, not quantity. . . . Dying early or late is of no consequence, dying well is. . . . Even if it is true that, while there is life there is hope, life is not to be bought at any cost.*

Seneca

# Chapter 13
# Euthanasia

E uthanasia is one of the more controversial, complex and difficult issues involving the dying. Euthanasia is the allowance or the inducement of a painless, quick death. Active euthanasia refers to acts in which one does something directly to end life when it would otherwise continue. Passive euthanasia refers to acts in which one refrains from doing something so that death will come quickly.

A major problem in the euthanasia controversy is the inclination toward simplistic attitudes and solutions. Since euthanasia involves moral, ethical, social, political, economic, and legal issues, many questions need to be considered before "right" decisions can be made.

1. Does a person have a constitutional or legal right to choose death? If so, is the right always in his best interests?

2. Does death by choice represent medicine's best answer to the difficult question of incurable and/or terminal illness?

3. Does the right to die sanction or encourage self-destruction impulses in people?

4. Does society have an investment in human life that overrides the individual and, conversely,

does the idea of "easy death" give society a dangerous weapon to regulate population?

5. Which is preferable, quantity or quality of life?

6. Is death always an enemy? Can death be a friend?

7. Can one assume any initiative in his dying? Can there be a stewardship of illness and death as well as a stewardship of health and life?

These questions and others are important considerations in making decisions regarding euthanasia. Just as each person's attitudes, behaviors, and dying processes are unique, so will be the decisions concerning euthanasia for the dying. Each case has its own special aspects and each needs to be dealt with on that basis. Firm, clear answers that apply equally to all persons are not possible.

However, there are some practical guidelines that can be helpful for all concerned in euthanasia situations.

1. Treat the person as a living human being until death, even when in a coma or unconscious. Something splendid may be going on.

2. Be honest with the dying.

3. Allow persons to participate in decisions concerning their care.

4. Listen to and accept a person's feelings about his death.

5. Respect a person's faith and belief system concerning life, death, and beyond.

6. Relieve pain and suffering.

7. Respect the person's choice concerning the way he prefers to die and the disposition of his body. The Living Will is helpful here.

8. Give the best possible overall care.

9. Utilize all available treatment resources and support persons.

10. Do not let a person die alone, if at all possible.

11. Hear out the concerns of loved ones, clergy, and physicians.

Even if all of these guidelines can be carried out, there still may be doubt about the rightness or wrongness of your care of the person and of your participation in his choices and/or the choices of others involved in the case. When all is said and done, probably the most any of us can do is to be sure that our thoughts, words, and deeds are motivated by love for the dying person. If such love is sincere and pure, we need have no guilt or remorse.

# A LIVING WILL

TO MY FAMILY, MY PHYSICIAN,
MY CLERGYMAN, MY LAWYER:

If the time comes when I can no longer take part in decisions for my own future, let this statement stand as the testament of my wishes:

If there is no reasonable expectation of my recovery from physical or mental or spiritual disability, I, _____ , request that I be allowed to die and not be kept alive by artificial means or heroic measures. Death is as much a reality as birth, growth, maturity, and old age — it is the one certainty. I do not fear death as much as I fear the indignity of deterioration, dependence, and hopeless pain. I ask that drugs be mercifully administered to me for terminal suffering even if they hasten the moment of death.

This request is made while I am in good health and spirits. Although this document is not legally binding, you who care for me will, I hope, feel morally bound to follow its mandates. I recognize it places a heavy burden of responsibility upon you, and it is with the intention of sharing that responsibility and of mitigating any feelings of guilt that this statement is made. Witnesses:

_____

_____

Signature

Date _____

(Sign this document in the presence of witnesses and give a copy to your family physician, attorney, pastor and a member of your family).

*Show me the manner in which a nation cares for its dead, and I will measure with mathematical exactness the tender mercies of its people, their respect for the laws of the land and their loyalty to high ideals.*

William E. Gladstone

*Mayhap a funeral among men is a wedding feast among the angels.*

Kahlil Gibran

*Under the wide and starry sky*
*Dig the grave and let me lie.*
*Glad did I live and gladly die,*
*And I laid me down with a will.*

*This be the verse you grave for me:*
*Here he lies where he longed to be;*
*Home is the sailor, home from the sea,*
*And the hunter home from the hill.*

Robert Louis Stevenson

# Chapter 14
# The Funeral

Since the beginning of human history, persons have honored their dead and expressed their grief through funeral services. Funeral customs vary widely and include many dimensions. Funerals involve religious, social, fraternal, civic and military organizations and are regulated by local, state and federal laws.

Today in America, the funeral and burial business is extensive. There is constant concern and competition among funeral directors, memorial societies, and other organizations associated with death over the value and cost of funerals and burials.

A complete funeral service usually involves:

1. Removing body to funeral home.

2. Embalming, preparing, and dressing the deceased.

3. Cosmetology, restorative art, hair dressing.

4. Counseling and arrangement of services.

5. Obtaining legal permits.

6. Notifying newspapers and fraternal organizations.

7. Preparing and filing death certificates.

8. Assisting with applications for Social Security and V.A. benefits.

9. Providing staff during calling hours and 24 hour on call availability.

10. Arranging and supervising funeral service, usually conducted by clergy.

11. Providing use of operating room.

12. Using funeral home for visitations and for the service.

13. Furnishing special equipment when needed.

14. Providing paraphernalia for religious, military, and fraternal rituals.

15. Providing hearse and limousine.

16. Printing and supplying paper and acknowledgement cards.

17. Providing a memorial register book.

There are some basic steps that need to be taken before the funerals by the family. Funeral directors help with these.

1. Phone funeral director and clergyman.

2. Arrange care for the survivor in deepest grief.

3. Meet with funeral director to discuss arrangements.

4. Establish date and hour of service and visitation.

5. Decide location of service.

6. Select cemetery lot if you don't have one.

7. Notify relatives, friends, neighbors, business associates.

8. Provide data for newspaper notices.

9. Select pallbearers.

10. Arrange for someone to be at home during visiting hours and time of funeral.

11. Plan what is to follow burial. Usually family and friends go to homestead and share a meal.

12. Arrange service with clergyman, if you desire to.

13. Arrange for transportation.

Funeral costs vary widely depending on the kind and extent of services and quality of casket. In addition to these, which are major expenses, there are other costs.

1. Cemetery plot.

2. Opening and closing of grave.

3. Vault, if required by cemetery.

4. Clergy honorarium (optional).

5. Clothing if deceased's own clothes are not used.

6. Classified obituaries for newspaper.

7. Certified copies of death certificate.

8. Headstone or grave marker.

Today more people are pre-arranging their funeral services. This practice generally saves money, reduces the stress of last minute decisions, enables family members to discuss their wishes, helps prepare all involved psychologically and enables them to be more in touch with their own death. Funeral directors are recommending this practice.

There are many ways to pre-plan your funeral or help a loved one plan. The following is one guide that can be helpful.

# LOOKING AHEAD
## A Guide to Help You and Those Who Survive You

This form has been devised to help you and your survivors deal with the difficult decisions that come with death. In addition to preventing practical problems and misunderstandings, completing this form enables you and your loved ones to be better prepared mentally and emotionally to face death.

I do do not wish to have unusual measures or artificial means used to sustain my life when death is imminent.

I do do not wish to give my eyes or other organs to another person for transplant purposes; I do do not wish to give my body for medical research or training. (In both cases authorization must be made in writing. Special forms are available for this purpose from various organizations.)

I do do not wish an autopsy to be performed if permission for it is requested.

At the time of my death, please notify those listed below. (List may include pastor, funeral home, relatives, employer, friends and co-workers, cemetery, unions and fraternal and professional organizations, Social Security office, Veterans Administration office, attorney, newspapers, insurance agent, etc.)

_____

Name & Identification    Telephone    Address (if needed)

_____

_____

_____

(Attach extra sheet if needed)

I wish earth burial ☐; mausoleum entombment ☐; cremation ☐, with ashes to be

_____

Cemetery name, location and lot numbers

_____

_____

Preferences regarding marker

_____

_____

I desire that a   funeral service   or a memorial service   be
held,  with   without   viewal of my body, at _____
_____ . Further plans for such a service have
been discussed with _____ and are attached
(include casketbearers, organist, vocalists, favorite music, and
type of service). I prefer that any memorial gifts be designated
for organizations and institutions most meaningful to me and
my family such as _____ .

BIOGRAPHICAL INFORMATION:

Born (place and date)

_____

Father's name _____

Mother's name _____

Date baptized _____

Date confimed _____

Church

_____

Place and date of marriages and to whom

_____

_____

Children (if not all listed on other side)

_____

_____

(Attach a brief biography, including schools, memberships,
places of employment, accomplishments, etc.)

VALUABLE RECORDS:

Location of birth certificate _____
Marriage certificate _____
Veteran's Identification No. _____
Location of discharge papers _____

VA office to notify _____

Social Security No. _____

Location of office _____

Location of will and/or trust _____

Location of safe deposit box _____

(Attach a list of other valuables — including stocks, bonds, deeds, etc.) Bank accounts (name, location, type) _____

_____

Pension benefits (employers to notify) _____

_____

_____

INSURANCE POLICIES:

| Company or Society | Policy or Contract No. | Amount | Agent or Representative |
|---|---|---|---|
| | | | |
| | | | |
| | | | |
| | | | |
| | | | |

Outstanding loans and credit obligations (attach dated listing and bring up to date each year).

These seem to be the wisest and most prudent decisions at this time. However, I expect my survivors to use good judgment in making necessary changes.

Signature _____ Date _____

Address _____

(Keep this form in a safe but accessible place and inform several people close to you of its existence. You may need to prepare extra copies.)

*It behooves the healers to quiet their minds enough to allow themselves to become a more total instrument of sensing than merely that which comes in through their senses or their intellect.*

Ram Dass

*Centering and quietness enable us to share in the power of God and resonate to the rhythms of life. In the stillness we gain a foretaste of life beyond, a foretaste that lies far beyond the reach of our intellect or so-called psychological awareness. It is in this space that we are prepared for the moment of death, for as we contemplate our being in silence, we also contemplate our non-being. If death comes to us as an unwelcome stranger, it will be in part because we have not experienced the silence of death in the stillness of our life.*

Louis Richard Batzler

*The reason people burn out as therapists, as healers, is because they are attached to whether the healing works or not and you can't play God. How do you know whether a person is supposed to be healed or whether they are supposed to die and why should you know?*

Ram Dass

# Chapter 15
# Stress and Burnout

Stress is a normal part of life; burnout is not. The challenge, therefore, is to understand and manage stress so that you can benefit from it rather than be destroyed by it. Essential to such understanding is the realization that there are many factors to be considered in the causes and management of stress. These include:

1. *Physical*
   a. Heredity
   b. Diet
   c. Weight
   d. Work
   e. Internal environment (disease, malformation, disability)
   f. External environment (pollution of air, water, sound)
   g. Exercise and rest, sleep, relaxation

2. *Mental and Emotional*
   a. Education
   b. Attitude (self-image, self-responsibility, self-awareness, self-control, self-discipline, self-determination)
   c. Life style
   d. Values, philosophy, belief systems
   e. Goals
   f. Work

g. Relationships (marriage, family, friends)

h. Financial situation

i. Significant changes (death, job, jail, home)

3. *Spiritual*

a. Religious training

b. Spiritual discipline and practice (personal, social)

c. Particular belief systems (morals, ethics, mores)

d. Reality of God in one's life

e. Harmony of thought, word, deed

f. Actualization of spiritual fruits (love, joy, peace, etc.)

g. Service to others

Death-related stresses, which are often the most intense, involve many of these factors. Most persons are not personally and continually dealing with death-related stresses. However, a sizeable number of professionals are involved with the dying and are exposed to many of the accompanying stresses. This chapter is primarily for those persons who deal daily or frequently with the dying and thus are more subject to the cumulative stress factors and resultant burnout.

One of the main reasons that stresses related to the dying are so intense for those in the healing profession is that the primary purpose of the health caretaker is curing, maintaining wellness and helping persons move toward a fuller life. With the dying, the caretaker is actually helping the patient to disengage from life. Thus there is an internal conflict within the caretaker at the onset of the terminal phase of the dying person.

Much of the information that follows is based on experiences of nurses working with the terminally ill, in intensive care units, emergency room, nursing homes, and also hospice personnel who are regularly involved with the dying and their families.

Any effective approach to stress management requires the recognition of the reality of the triune nature of persons — body, mind-emotions, spirit — and considers all of these aspects of personhood in dealing with stress. To omit any one of these aspects is to diminish the possibilities for preventing or healing distress.

The inseparable relation between body, mind, and spirit indicates that there is constant interaction between the three aspects. To deal with a stress factor in one means that the other two aspects of the self also need to be considered. Usually the stress factor is dominant in one aspect and that aspect becomes the main focus of attention. In the classifications below, each of the three aspects of self is considered in conjunction with the other two and some basic suggestions offered for dealing with stresses.

1. *Body*, mind, spirit

   a. *Exercise*. Regular and disciplined bodily exercise is most important in handling stress. Research and experiments in physical exercise programs reveal the benefits to all of the body systems through exercise. Stretching (hatha yoga), calisthenics, aerobics, strengthening exercises (weight-lifting) each have a part in improving bodily health and mental well-being. Coupled with these exercises are the factors of rest and relaxation which facilitate the needed rhythms of the body systems. Rest and relaxation might include withdrawing from the burdens of the day by taking a walk or catnap. Mini-vacations, long week-ends and half-days are other possibilities.

In all physical exercises, it is important to harmonize them with mental attitudes. When exercising, you need to have positive mental attitudes toward those exercises. To do exercises which you do not like is to create an antagonism between body and mind and thus produce more stress. There are more than enough enjoyable physical exercises from which to choose.

b. *Relaxation*. When thinking of stress, relaxation often comes to mind. Relaxation is more than lying or sitting comfortably. Real relaxation involves mental activity of releasing troubling thoughts, stilling and centering the mind, as well as measured breathing and posturing the body. There are many ways to induce relaxation such as visualizing pleasant scenes, rhythmically breathing, imaging, reduced activity and motion, systematically relaxing each part of the body, biofeedback, self-hypnosis, counting, repeated affirmations or mantras. A very beneficial relaxer is reflexology, sometimes called zone therapy or press point therapy. This is a special technique of pressure and massage on the feet to stimulate glands and organs, alleviate pain and emotional stress and promote circulation. This technique is based on the belief that nerve-like connecting pathways to all parts of the body are closest to the surface and easiest to locate in the feet and that pressure and massage properly administered will relax and normalize bodily functions.

Numerous relaxation exercises can be found in books, tapes and records.[1] These can help you discover what works best for you and also enable you to develop your own method. For those who have strenuous and high stress activity, frequent brief periods of relaxation are recommended. Regularity of relaxation is important. The body has its own wisdom and if you are attuned to the body, you will know when and how to relax, release and rely.

c. *Diet*. More and more emphasis is being placed on the significance of the food you eat in the prevention and handling of stress. Diet, or proper nutrition, is one of the most important factors in promoting and maintaining bodily health and mental and emotional well-being. There are many good diets and many approaches as to how we should eat. Good nutrition requires a knowledge of the basic wholesome and unwholesome foods and disciplined practice in eating the wholesome ones. Good nutrition also includes moderation in eating, some fasting, enjoying your food, eating slowly and in congenial environments, being grateful for and blessing your food and having a positive attitude toward eating that coincides with your total life philosophy. The food you eat, or don't eat, is often the major cause of your diseases and discomforts.

2. *Mind*, body, spirit.

   a. *Values clarification*. Much undue stress is caused by confusion or the absence of clear values. The many forces in our society that seek to win your commitment and claim your energies and resources can cause consternation, confusion and chaos in your mental and emotional life. To clarify and firm up your belief systems and values, to establish priorities and actualize them, eliminates much internal and external conflict. Often you can help to clarify your values by having a mentor, a special friend, who might be older and wiser, who can give you honest, helpful feedback. There are many values clarification exercises available.[2]

   b. *Goal setting*. Goal setting is closely related to values clarification. Having goals enables you to focus and center on that which is desired and meaningful. Setting goals facilitates intentional living and reduces stress caused by ambivalence and aimlessness.

   c. *Affirmations*. An affirmation is a brief, positive statement intended to motivate, firm up and activate beliefs and attitudes. Affirmations can create healing energies in the body, produce beneficial effects in the subconscious, facilitate peace and harmony and improve your self-image and confidence. Affirmations are an important factor in establishing positive attitudes which contribute so much to wholeness.[3]

d. *Positive attitudes*. Positive attitudes are extensions and expansions of affirmations. Basic positive attitudes are self-responsibility, self-awareness, self-control, self-discipline, self-respect, self-confidence. If you can seriously and successfully integrate these positive dynamics of selfhood, stress-related diseases and difficulties will be greatly decreased or eliminated.[4]

e. *Guided imagery*. This is a variation of the affirmation and positive attitude in which you, in a relaxed and meditative state, visualize situations or conditions as you want them to be. It is using your imagination to focus energies and intentions which can be catalysts for transformation. Guided imagery is helpful in preventing depression, stress and in curing disease.

f. *Changing routine*. This is a simple and effective way to deal with stress that is often associated with your work or life patterns. Much distress comes from boredom, routine and conformity, all of which hinder the creative process which is so important to healthy and meaningful living. Too frequently you get into ruts (a rut is a grave with the ends knocked out) which drag you into depressive states. Altering your routines can open new doors to areas of life that are beautiful and bountiful.

g. *Journaling*. Journaling is a method that can be used to deal with stress. This is a process in which you record significant events in your daily life (or weekly) and then periodically reflect on these recordings. What this does is to reveal in specific ways how you deviate from or conform to your goals, intentions and priorities and identifies stress points. It is taking inventory of your life in order to clarify, center, control and be creative.

h. *Humor and laughter*. Humor and laughter are very closely related to physical, mental and emotional health. Muscle tone, diaphragmatic activity, physiological arousal and relaxation of body and mind are results of humor and laughter. All of these dynamics can be stress preventors, relievers and facilitators of healing processes. Humor and laughter might also be a means of pain control and a way of establishing or restoring communication with self and others.[5]

i. *Music*. Music is the universal langauge that touches and moves human beings at many levels. Music reveals and brings to us beauty, joy, peace and power. It stimulates the imagination, comforts the mind and spirit, increases awareness, relaxes body and mind, inspires the heart, excites the emotions and helps to increase creativity. Music can be used in many ways to facilitate healing, renew life and promote wholeness of body, mind and spirit.

The dying person can find comfort and hope through music. Music can heal memories, renew communication with others and self and give strength and courage to face death. There are instances where music has brought persons out of a coma, enabled persons to speak who had become mute and prevented suicide. Sometimes the combination of words and music together are effective helps for the dying.[6]

j. *Dreams*. Dreams are one of your greatest stress relievers. Most persons do not realize or utilize this source of information and help. Dreams can shed light on your unresolved conflicts, unfulfilled desires, unsolved problems and confront you with your fears, frustrations, failures and sorrows. Dreams affirm that which is good and positive in you and provide motivation and inspiration as well as specific guidelines for action. Dreams tell us much about ourselves and thus provide valuable information, insights and perspectives for living well. Repetitive dreams are especially important and need to be heeded.

3. *Spirit*, mind body.

a. *Love*. Love is the greatest factor in wholeness. To give and to receive love is the essence of your humanity. God is love and when you love, you experience and express God in your life. Where God is experienced and expressed, there peace, joy, and wholeness prevail. Love is the mainspring of existence, the great healer and the revealer of truth. Love does not prevent stress, but transforms it to beautiful, creative, constructive and consecrated purposes.

b. *Morals and ethics*. Throughout history there have been many moral and ethical beliefs and systems. These usually come into being to enable individuals and societies to live fruitfully in community. Morals and ethics constitute frame-works out of which persons, groups and institutions can function, provide norms and limits of behavior and protect rights. Unfortunately, morals and ethics sometimes become vehicles of control and manipulation. In terms of stress management, morals and ethics can be valuable motivators and guides for healthy living. If you have clear, firm moral and ethical beliefs and behavior and you can be reasonably flexible, tolerant and understanding of others' belief systems, then stress problems should be less.

c. *Spiritual exercises*. Just as the body and mind need nurture and exercise, so does the human spirit. Many of our physical, mental and emotional distresses are the result of little or no spiritual life. There are many spiritual exercises you can do, either alone or with others. Several of these are described in Chapter 16, *Exercises to Help You Deal With Your Own Death and the Death of Others*. Spiritual maturity is important for all persons. It is especially so for the dying and their caretakers.

*Now, it turns out, that the optimum strategy for heal-ing — for consciousness — is to be in the moment — to be very clear, very present, very tuned — listening, quieting, deepening, opening presence. That's the optimum strategy for living; it is also the absolute optimum strategy for dying.*

Ram Dass

*It is only in the face of death that man's self is born.*

St. Augustine

*The present hour is the descending God, and all things obey; all the past exists to it as subordinate; all the future is contained in it. . . . By lowly listening, omniscience is for me. By faithfully receiving, omnipo-tence is for me.*

Ralph Waldo Emerson

# Chapter 16

# Exercises to Help in Dealing With Your Own Death and the Death of Others

Just as each person dies uniquely, so does each person who works with the dying react uniquely to the dying person. There are many ways in which caretakers can prepare for coping with their stresses of intense involvement with the dying and with the death saturation syndromes that often develop.

Today more attention is being given to this problem, and institutions and agencies that care for the sick and dying are beginning to take steps toward helping the helpers. These steps include formal training in the care of the dying by schools of nursing, hospice organizations, medical schools and seminaries; in-service and continuing education seminars and workshops; inter-disciplinary staff meetings in hospitals; psychological and psychiatric support for staff who care for the dying.

Much of the preparation can be done by the individuals themselves. The exercises in this chapter are some of the ways that caretakers for the dying — professional or nonprofessional — can become more in touch with their own death, thereby helping themselves and their patients.

Despite all of our preparation, however, it must be noted that no one is ever fully emotionally prepared for a death, whether the death be that of a patient, friend or close relative. This is especially true of sudden and unexpected deaths. This realization helps us to be free to react from our deepest levels and intense needs, to not be ashamed or afraid to grieve in any way — in a word, to be fully human when death enters our own circle of life.

# I

## Death and the Self

These suggestions are intended to help you see the naturalness of death, feel more comfortable with death language, concepts and experiences, eliminate death-related fears and develop positive attitudes and feelings toward your own death.

1. Examine your fears and superstitions about death in general and your own death in particular.

2. Deal with the fact of death daily through brief reflections, memento, obituary, etc. This means, each day, to be aware of and to accept the reality of death as part of the reality of life.

3. Look at your relationship to the material world by observing your attitudes and feelings toward your possessions — how you obtain, use, share, dispose of them. What are your most precious possessions? What would you do if you inherited a million dollars?

4. Reflect on the meaning of and your relationship to time. What is eternity? Is any death untimely? How long does it take to fulfill a life's purpose? What would you do if you knew you had one month to live, or unlimited time?

5. Study some good writings about death and life after death, especially scripture. Discuss death-related issues such as abortion, euthanasia, etc.

6. Examine your relationships with others in the context of death; e.g., imagining that the persons you are presently relating to will be dead tomorrow or very soon.

7. Make special efforts to develop sensitive acquaintances with those who are dying, such as the terminally and chronically ill, the elderly. Move toward rather than away from the dying.

8. Offer prayers for the dead. As your list increases, consciousness of the naturalness of death increases and the veil between the two worlds is less foreboding.

9. Attend funerals and be with the bereaved. Your presence, even in silence, is power for you and the grieving.

10. Make your will and be open in helping others do this.

11. Do some thinking about your own suicide. This helps to focus on what you consider is intolerable in your life and aids you in dealing with that.

12. Consider how you can make your present life worse. Knowing what you don't want sometimes helps you judge how close you are to what you do want.

13. Try some disability exercises such as simulated blindness, deafness, dumbness, immobility, etc., for a period of hours or days.

14. Participate in some death-centered programs, e.g., self-awareness groups, hospice, Make Today Count, Widow to Widow, etc.

15. Make a list of persons in your life who have died and reopen the relationship by raising to new levels. Note that though these relationships are completed, they are not over because these

persons still live on in you. Those who have died can be important teachers of the meaning of relationships.

16. Reflect on death in your spiritual journey and faith, especially noting the significance of resurrection in your thoughts, words and deeds.

## II

### Becoming Aware of Feelings

Relax, close your eyes, visualize and imagine someone you love is dying. First, consider your patient is dying and get in touch with your feelings in your role as a nurse or other caretaker. Next, consider a very dear family member or friend is dying and be aware of these feelings. Now compare and contrast the feelings and try to discover the differences and then notice how the differences make you feel.

This exercise helps you to realize the dilemmas and confusion you often face in dealing with the dying and the need to affirm your love and care, which is primarily what every dying person needs and wants.

## III

### Who am I?

This question, asked since the beginning of time, is helpful in realizing who you have been, who you now are, and who you yet can be. This exercise is best done in pairs, but can be done alone. Simply ask the question, "Who am I?", and then begin to answer all of the *who's* you have been and now are, e.g., girl, sister, daughter, mother, etc. When done in pairs, the question, "Who are you?", is asked and each partner takes turns in answering. Each answer you give has many ramifications and the exercise enables you to realize the many aspects, functions and contributions of your life. Also, in answering who you have been and now are, reveals to you your unfulfilled potential and who you yet can be. This helps you to center, define and develop goals for more intentional living. Your balance is reflected to the patient.

If done with care and discernment, this exercise might also be used with a dying person. Dying persons often feel dejected and depressed because they think their life has no meaning. By getting them to see their past accomplishments, relationships and ways they have influenced others and how they can influence persons in their future can help them cope with their dying.

## IV

## What Does Your Name Mean to You?

One of the distresses the dying encounter is the loss of identity. Identity is often associated with one's name. This simple exercise can have profound implications. It is most productive when done in groups where individuals pair off and ask the above question of each other for five minutes. Then the answers are discussed among the total group.

What this exercise does is to help participants look at their identity, roots, relationships and the significance of words. Some lives have been changed when persons have reflected on the meaning of their names. This exercise is valuable for self-examination, self-realization and for helping others in their journey toward selfhood in living and in dying.

# V

## Looking

We learn much by being still and observing. Choose a partner, sit facing her and look directly at her for five minutes. In this eyeball to eyeball encounter, you may do whatever you feel like doing except talk. This confrontation often brings to the surface hidden emotions and deep feelings, interesting insights about ourselves and others, and tests our ability to "stay with" a person. It can be an intensive experience that opens up new levels of awareness and provides ways for becoming better helpers for those who are dying and in distress.

# VI

## Life Line

This exercise confronts you with the reality of life and death by helping you to see where you are in your life line.

Draw a horizontal line across the paper. Put a dot at each end. Over the left dot put O which represents your birth. The dot on your right represents your death. Over the right dot, put the estimated date of your death, based on the number of years you think you will live.

On the line, place a dot which represents where you are right now in your life's journey. Write today's date over this dot. Reflect on this diagram and then ascertain how you feel and what you think.

This exercise can be done in groups or individually.

# VII

## Facing Death

### Thoughts and Feelings about My Own Death

This exercise, when done in a group, and then discussed has endless possibilities. Each question has within it a number of other questions. Thus in I A, if your answer is *so, so,* you might ask why has your life not been *real good.* Or look at II A. This question poses a prior question. Before you can answer what happens to "ME" in death, you need to consider who is "ME" right now.

Directions: Please answer the following as truthfully as possible. Indicate your first impression. Do not try to find false clues or psychological tricks for there are none here. There are no right or wrong answers — only your answers.

I. *What is Life?*

    A. Has life been good to you?
       ☐ Real good; ☐ So, so; ☐ Not so good.

    B. Have you already accomplished your life's goals?
       ☐ Most of them; ☐ About half; ☐ Less than half.

    C. Is life interesting to you?
       ☐ Mostly so; ☐ Once in a while; ☐ Seldom.

    D. Has God been fair to you?
       ☐ In most cases; ☐ Once in a while He isn't;
       ☐ Seldom.

    E. Would you like to relive your life?
       ☐ Most of it; ☐ About half; ☐ I like it the way it has been.

    F. Are you usually happy?
       ☐ Most of the time; ☐ Seldom; ☐ A good portion;
       ☐ Half and half.

    G. Does your religious faith contribute to your happiness?
       ☐ Major part of it; ☐ Sometimes; ☐ Never.

H. How often do you feel you would have chosen another vocation if you had it to do over again:
☐ Seldom; ☐ Most of the time; ☐ More times than not; ☐ Never.

I. Have you the feeling that God has punished you in life?
☐ Never; ☐ Once in a while; ☐ Often.

II. *Religion and Life*

A. What happens to "ME" in death?

B. What does death hold for you?
☐ Limbo; ☐ An end; ☐ An adventure; ☐ An escape.

C. How does your religious orientation fit in with death? (50 words or less)

III. *Social Considerations about Death*

A. At what age do you expect to die? —————————

B. Where do you expect to die?
☐ In your own bed
☐ In an accident situation
☐ In a hospital
☐ In a nursing home

C. What person would you like to have with you at the time of death?
☐ Closest relative of my choice
☐ Any person (e.g., doctor, nurse, friend, etc.)
☐ Clergyman
☐ No one

D. What person would you feel free to talk with concerning death?
☐ Closest relative of my choice
☐ Physician
☐ Clergyman
☐ Friend
☐ No one

E. How do you expect to die?
☐ During a surgical procedure
☐ From lingering illness
☐ From natural causes
☐ In an accident
☐ From a heart attack

F. In terms of your closest human relationship, do you desire
   - ☐ To die before him/her
   - ☐ To die with him/her
   - ☐ To die after him/her

G. Have you made a will?  ☐ yes  ☐ no

H. In terms of the person, whose death would be most difficult for you?
   1. Why would this person's death be so devastating?
   2. Would this person's death affect your life's goals?
   3. Would this person's death thrust an inconvenience on you?
   4. How much does this person contribute to your self-image?
   5. What defense mechanisms would you expect to use to overcome the loss of such a person?
   6. What do you think would be the extent of your grief reaction?
   7. Has this person ever talked with you about the possibility of his/her death?
   8. Would you want to be with this person when he/she died?

IV. *Evaluation of Self-Image*

   A. Having completed the previous questions, write below a short obituary for yourself for the time when you expect to die.

   B. Write a eulogy for yourself. Set it in the time frame you have projected for your death.

   C. Write your own epitaph. Reflect on what it says about your life. Do this in less than 50 words.

# VIII

## Facing a Patient's Death

## My Thoughts and Feelings about a Patient's Death as a Key to Thinking and Feeling about My Own Death

Directions: Answer the following as truthfully as possible. Indicate your first impression. Then reflect on your answers and/or decisions with others.

1. How often has caring for an incurable, terminally ill patient made you feel:

    A. Discouraged?
    ___ 1. Almost always
    ___ 2. Occasionally
    ___ 3. Seldom
    ___ 4. Never

    B. Depressed?
    ___ 1. Almost always
    ___ 2. Occasionally
    ___ 3. Seldom
    ___ 4. Never

    C. Angry?
    ___ 1. Almost always
    ___ 2. Occasionally
    ___ 3. Seldom
    ___ 4. Never

    D. Satisfied and fulfilled?
    ___ 1. Almost always
    ___ 2. Occasionally
    ___ 3. Seldom
    ___ 4. Never

2. Certain kinds of dying patients elicit different feelings. How would you feel about caring for the following?

    A. A newborn infant?
    ___ 1. Wouldn't mind
    ___ 2. Somewhat uncomfortable
    ___ 3. Very uncomfortable
    ___ 4. Unable to cope

B. A young child?
___ 1. Wouldn't mind
___ 2. Somewhat uncomfortable
___ 3. Very uncomfortable
___ 4. Unable to cope

C. An adolescent?
___ 1. Wouldn't mind
___ 2. Somewhat uncomfortable
___ 3. Very uncomfortable
___ 4. Unable to cope

D. A young adult?
___ 1. Wouldn't mind
___ 2. Somewhat uncomfortable
___ 3. Very uncomfortable
___ 4. Unable to cope

E. A mother with young children at home?
___ 1. Wouldn't mind
___ 2. Somewhat uncomfortable
___ 3. Very uncomfortable
___ 4. Unable to cope

F. A father with a young family?
___ 1. Wouldn't mind
___ 2. Somewhat uncomfortable
___ 3. Very uncomfortable
___ 4. Unable to cope

G. A middle-aged person?
___ 1. Wouldn't mind
___ 2. Somewhat uncomfortable
___ 3. Very uncomfortable
___ 4. Unable to cope

H. An elderly person?
___ 1. Wouldn't mind
___ 2. Somewhat uncomfortable
___ 3. Very uncomfortable
___ 4. Unable to cope

I. A very old person?
___ 1. Wouldn't mind
___ 2. Somewhat uncomfortable
___ 3. Very uncomfortable
___ 4. Unable to cope

3. When should a patient with a terminal illness be told that he is dying?

___ A. As soon as possible after the diagnosis is certain
___ B. The news should be broken to the patient slowly over an extended period of time as the illness progresses
___ C. A patient should be told only when in the last stages of dying and death is imminent
___ D. A patient should never be told that he is dying, only that he has a serious illness
___ E. Only when he asks

4. When a terminally ill patient brings up the topic of his death or dying, what is your honest, inner reaction?

___ A. It makes me feel anxious and uncomfortable
___ B. It makes me feel somewhat uncomfortable
___ C. I feel somewhat relieved that the patient has brought up the topic
___ D. I have never been involved in such a situation

5. When a patient who has a terminal illness bluntly asks you if he is dying and his physician does not want the patient to know, what do you usually do:

___ A. Avoid the question and distract the patient in some way
___ B. Reassure the patient that he is not dying, just ill
___ C. Tell the patient that the question can be answered only by his physician and that you are not in a position to tell him
___ D. Ask the patient why he brought up the question. Try to get him to talk about his feelings, and sit and listen to what he has to say
___ E. Say you don't know
___ F. Tell him the truth

6. When physicians have refused to tell your patients that they were dying, how many of these patients nevertheless clearly knew of and referred to their impending death?

___ A. Very few, less than 10%
___ B. A small proportion, up to 25%
___ C. About half
___ D. A large proportion, up to 75%
___ E. A very large proportion, up to 90%

_____ F. Every one, without exception

_____ G. Have not cared for enough dying patients to estimate

7. In your own experience, how many terminally ill patients continued to deny, until the very end, that they would die?

_____ A. Very few, less than 10%

_____ B. A small proportion, up to 25%

_____ C. About half

_____ D. A large proportion, up to 75%

_____ E. A very large proportion, up to 90%

_____ F. Every one, without exception

_____ G. Have not cared for enough dying patients to estimate

8. When is it usually more difficult to care for a terminally ill patient?

_____ A. When the patient has been told he is dying

_____ B. When the patient has not been told he is dying

9. When the family of a dying patient comes to you, how difficult is it for you to deal with them?

_____ A. Usually very difficult

_____ B. Difficult with some but not with others

_____ C. Usually I have no difficulties

10. How do you feel about the following:

A. Withholding all life-sustaining treatment for dying patients who don't want it?

_____ 1. In favor

_____ 2. Mixed feelings, slightly in favor

_____ 3. Mixed feelings, slightly against

_____ 4. Against

B. Mercy killing or active euthanasia for dying patients who request it?

_____ 1. In favor

_____ 2. Mixed feelings, slightly in favor

_____ 3. Mixed feelings, slightly against

_____ 4. Against

C. Maintaining terminally ill patients by extraordinary means in order to study their disease?

_____ 1. In favor

_____ 2. Mixed feelings, slightly in favor

_____ 3. Mixed feelings, slightly against
_____ 4. Against

11. Do you believe that if a terminally ill patient is suffering beyond endurance and pleads for an end to his life, he should be given the means to do so?

_____ A. Yes
_____ B. It depends on the patient and on the circumstances
_____ C. No

12. What is your predominant feeling about having to care for the body of a patient after death?

_____ A. Fear
_____ B. Distaste
_____ C. Acceptance of necessity of this task
_____ D. No special feeling

13. Whose death produced the most profound effect on your attitude toward death and dying?

_____ A. Grandparent
_____ B. Parent
_____ C. Brother or sister
_____ D. Spouse
_____ E. Son or daughter
_____ F. Friend
_____ G. Patient
_____ H. Never had such an experience
_____ I. Other (please specify) _____

14. What does death mean to you?

_____ A. Reincarnation
_____ B. Being with God
_____ C. An ending of earthly life but with the continued individual existence of the soul
_____ D. A joining of the soul with a universal consciousness
_____ E. A kind of endless sleep
_____ F. The end of all experiences; a total and irreversible blotting out of existence
_____ G. Something other than the above (please specify)
_____

15. What has the greatest influence in shaping your present attitudes toward death and dying?

_____ A. Religious teachings

___ B. Reading certain books and articles about death and
dying
___ C. Conversation with terminally ill patients
___ D. Conversation with a person whose wisdom I respect
___ E. Coping with the death of someone close
___ F. Introspection about my own death
___ G. Other (please specify) _____

16. In learning how to deal with the emotional and psychological problems of dying patients and their families, what
has been your one best source of helpful advice and information?

___ A. Classes at nursing school
___ B. Books and magazine articles
___ C. An experienced, helpful staff member
___ D. Staff discussions
___ E. Working and talking with dying patients and learning
from them
___ F. Seminars or workshops on death and dying
___ G. Other (please specify) _____

17. How confident do you feel in your ability to provide tech-
nical care to terminally ill patients?

___ A. Not at all confident
___ B. Slightly confident
___ C. Mostly confident
___ D. Very confident

18. How confident do you feel about your ability to manage
the psychological needs of terminally ill patients?

___ A. Not at all confident
___ B. Slightly confident
___ C. Mostly confident
___ D. Very confident

143

# IX

## Life After Death

### A Thinking and Feeling Experience about Life After Death

Your responses are +, −, or 0, depending on whether you think and feel positively (yes) about the statement (+), negatively (no) (−), or aren't sure (maybe) (0).

1. My life continues forever after death.

2. I fear death.

3. I shall maintain a recognizable identity after death.

4. I shall be able to communicate with loved ones who are still in the body after I die.

5. I believe that I shall reincarnate.

6. God utterly destroys the wicked after death.

7. The manner in which I live now will affect my life after death.

8. Suicide is sometimes the right thing to do.

9. Prayers for the departed are valid and good.

10. My view of what happens after death has an important influence on my relationships to those who are closest to me in this life now.

11. I believe that euthanasia is right.

12. I believe that life after death has been proven.

13. I believe that there is development and progress after death.

14. I shall meet and recognize persons of repute and those of earlier generations after death.

15. Persons who die mentally sick will go into the next life mentally ill.

16. My relationship to God now is important for life after death.

17. I shall be united with a loved one after death, even if he or she had no specific religious faith in this life.

18. I wish to have my body cremated.

19. I want to survive after death.

20. Unborn babies survive and grow after death.

21. I wish to have my body donated to medical science.

# X

## Examining Your Broad Life Goals

Most of your attitudes and actions are directly related to efforts to accomplish life goals. To have goals and to work toward achieving them, help give meaning, purpose, and value to life. These qualities are important in dealing with your own death and the death of others.

The following represent common life goals. Rank the items on this list in terms of your own values and priorities. One represents the most important, thirteen the least important. After you have done this, reflect on your choices in light of the fact of your own death. You might also want to discuss your answers with others.

RANKING

☐ Affection — to obtain and share companionship and affection

☐ Duty — to commit myself to what I call duty

☐ Expertness — to become an authority

☐ Independence — to have freedom of thought and action

☐ Leadership — to become influential and capable

☐ Parenthood — to raise a fine family — to have heirs

☐ Pleasure — to enjoy life — to be happy and content

☐ Power — to have control of others and events

☐ Prestige — to become well known and have status

☐ Security — to have a secure and stable position

☐ Self-Realization — to optimize personal development and be fulfilled

☐ Service — to contribute to the well-being of others

☐ Wealth — to earn a great deal of money and have many possessions

# XI

## Life Inventory

The recognition of meaningful experiences and unfulfilled desires and goals can clarify your values and motivate you to action. Taking inventory of your life is one way to do this and is helpful in dealing with death-related stresses.

The following are some basic starters.

1. Peak experiences I have had

2. Peak experiences I would like to have

3. What I do well

4. What I do poorly

5. What I would like to stop doing

6. What I would like to start doing now

7. What I would like to learn to do well

8. Values I want to actualize

Write what first comes to mind. Do not be concerned about overlap or duplication in your answer. You might want to talk your responses into a recorder and then listen to yourself or have a close friend ask the question which you will answer in writing.

# XII

## Mantra Or Holy Sentence

The mantra or holy sentence is a form of creative sound in which dormant forces of the soul are awakened. Like symbols, these words and sounds get past the conscious into the subconscious mind, establishing contact with the inner resources, thereby enabling you to experience deeper inspiration and more intensive illumination which help you to better confront death.

The sentence or words are to be repeated or chanted aloud for a number of times while in a quiet place and in a relaxed state. This exercise can be done alone or in a group.

The following sentences are suggestions. You can form your own sentence or word.

1. I am God's perfect child.

2. God, I love you more than myself, and I love myself only for you.

3. The kingdom of God is within me.

4. God is in me, through me, with me and for me; where God is, no imperfection can exist.

5. God is love and because I love, I dwell in God and God dwells in me.

6. I have passed from death to life because I love others.

7. With God, all is possible.

8. Christ is in me and I am in Christ.

9. God gives me perfect peace when I stay my mind on Him.

10. God is my shepherd, my refuge, my light. I shall not fear nor want.

## XIII

## Healing Of The Memories

Your difficulty in facing death may stem from a painful memory of your near or distant past. This exercise can help you heal the memory and alleviate regret, guilt, fear, or other negative forces that interfere with your present proper functioning in death-related situations.

1. Relax and visualize your spiritual master by your side.

2. Begin to walk back in time with your spiritual master, week by week, year by year, until you come to the person, place, or situation that needs healing.

3. At this space in your memory, strongly image your spiritual master with you. Feel his forgiving love permeating the memory scene; see him touching or embracing those needing healing; hear any words he offers of renewal, healing, and hope.

4. Experience any other feeling of renewal that may appear and then thank God for the healing that has taken place.

5. Accept and affirm the healing. Arise with joy and confidence.

# XIV

## Lotus Meditation

Meditation is basically a spiritual discipline or technique which enables you to actualize more of your potential, enlarge and enrich your capacity to love, expand your consciousness and sensitize your spirit to a greater awareness of and appreciation for God, others, and self. The realization of these values in your life is important in confronting your death.

The following meditation is one of many that can help you.

1. Relax and visualize a many-petaled lotus flower. Choose a subject (e.g., love, a person, a situation, etc.) and fix your attention on that subject, which is to form the center of the lotus. Then visualize one petal opening from the center and let this petal represent an aspect of the subject. For example, if Jesus is chosen as the center, let the first petal represent his love. Reflect on his love for a few moments and then go back to the center and let another petal open. This time, let the second petal represent another aspect of Jesus, e.g., his wisdom. Reflect on his wisdom. Repeat this process for as many petals as you can. When you finish, you will have had an intensive and comprehensive experience of feeling and thinking concerning the chosen subject. If you choose a dying person as the subject of your meditation, you will be able to bring forth numerous positive aspects of his life and thereby help him, especially in those despondent episodes when he sees no value to his life in his past, present, or future.

# XV

## Role Playing

There are many role playing situations that you can devise that will help you with specific questions and concerns that the dying raise. These can be done in pairs or larger groups. The following are some examples.

1. Assume that the doctor, family, and you know that the patient is dying, but he has not yet been told. The patient than asks you earnestly and directly, "Am I dying?"

2. The dying patient is anguishing over the lack of information and attention from the doctor. You experience this anguish and pain also as a nurse and feel the need to confront the doctor.

3. The patient, aware of his dying and needing to ventilate and get some comfort through dialogue asks, "How would you feel if you were dying?"

4. The dying patient, a professed atheist, expresses obvious fears about his death. Role play your responses.

5. A patient has just died, either in the emergency room or on the unit. You are on duty and have the responsibility of informing the family by telephone. How do you communicate this?

*I am convinced that the soul is indestructible, and
that its activity will continue through eternity. It is like
the sun, which to our eyes seems to set at night, but has
in reality only gone to diffuse its light elsewhere.*

Johann Wolfgang von Goethe

*O Lord!
If I worship you from fear of hell,
cast me into hell.
If I worship you from desire for paradise,
deny me paradise.*

Rabia (Sufi Saying)

*Whatever is here, that is there;
What is there, the same is here.
He who seeth here as different,
Meeteth death after death.*

Katha Upanishad

*A man should be able to say he has done his best to
form a conception of life after death, or to create some
image of it. Not to have done so is a vital loss.*

Carl Jung

*But the souls of the righteous are in the hand of God,
and there shall no torment touch them. In the sight of
the unwise they seemed to die: and their departure is
taken for misery, and their going from us to be utter
destruction: but they are in peace.*

Wisdom of Solomon 3:1-3

# Chapter 17
# Life After Death

Belief in life after death is important for the dying and for the living. Sometimes the importance is not always acknowledged or overtly expressed, but theological, philosophical, psychological, and psychical writings generally affirm that some belief in life after death is valuable in coping with impending death and also in providing a framework out of which persons formulate many of their attitudes and life styles.

Since life after death is a controversial subject and one which does not lend itself readily to scientific study and proof, you need to recognize that the best reasoned research on the subject spells out possibilities rather than certainties. Thus a realistic approach to the issue of life after death requires examining the various possible theories and explanations with openness and no prejudging.

In considering the beliefs that state individual awareness and consciousness extend beyond this earthly life, it is important to differentiate the concepts and contexts of these beliefs.

1. *Simple survival* indicates that something which is recognizably your consciousness will survive your physical death.

2. *Immortality* means that your "self," "soul,"

"spirit," "essential you" will continue to exist for an infinite time into the future.

3. *Eternal life* refers to the inner self, the true "I" which exists timelessly and is an expression, a part of Eternal Being. Eternal life asserts that the awareness and consciousness which is you now can ascend beyond the limits of time altogether.

Theology, philosophy, psychology, mythology, archeology, thanatology, and other disciplines reveal that virtually all civilizations and cultures evidence some belief in life after death. However, beliefs in the specific form and activity of the afterlife vary widely.

In the earliest cultures, life after death is regarded not as a matter of speculation, conjecture, hope or fear, but as a practical "certainty." Much of this "certainty" comes from the primitive's observations of nature — the waxing and waning of the moon, animals shedding skins, caterpillar and butterfly, the seasons. In observing the life-death-life cycles of nature and seeing himself as a part of nature, man thereby simply concludes that he, too, will undergo such a process. Early folklore reinforced this belief by telling of spirits of the deceased haunting landscapes, special places, and animals.

These early views of life after death do not seem to be inspired by ethical, moral or religious motives, but rather were an idealization of present conditions, e.g., happy hunting grounds or perpetual summers with no nights. One's lot after death was not determined by reward or retribution, but by natural forces and processes.

The oldest clearly formulated beliefs in life after death appear in early Egyptian civilization (c. 2000-

1600 B.C.) where preoccupation with the afterlife is seen in texts and tombs. Pharoahs are often identified with mythical gods who, by entering into cosmic cycles, do not experience decay. The afterlife is one of hope and death is a passage to rebirth, cyclical but unending. Judgment, retribution, immortality, and reincarnation are a part of Egyptian eschatology.

Belief in life after death in Indo-Iranian civilizations has taken shape in many forms and stages. In Eastern thought, life is not restricted in its meaning to the span of life between birth and death. Life is a process that goes on beyond the moment of death and a key purpose of life in the present is liberation from suffering. Life before, life now and life to come are inseparably related and how this relationship is spelled out is seen in the law of karma and in the belief in an indefinite series of rebirths. Salvation comes in the discovery and identification with Brahma, the basis of all reality. Eastern soteriology is not so much concerned with the whole man as we usually conceive him (body, mind, soul) but with his immortal component.

Iranian eschatology emphasizes the importance of the ethical life here and the fact that a future life is needed for the fulfillment of honor and virtue. Later Iranian beliefs stress resurrection and judgment and allude to universal immortality. Man is set free when evil is overcome.

Early Greek beliefs spoke of Hades as a common abode of the departed without regard to moral distinctions. The soul is a shade with no consciousness or will. In Homeric poems, the soul is a relic of a ghostly double with no element of value to look forward to. The idea of a future life was largely inoperative. Emphasis was on this world now.

The main principle of the Olympian religions, the popular faith of Greece, was the gulf between humans and the gods. However, the Orphic brotherhoods and mystery religions emphasized the mystical union with the gods so that life beyond becomes a continuing communion with God. Gradually the belief includes the reward and punishment dynamic and an intermediate state after death.

Plato spoke of the primacy and the divine origin of the soul which is one's real self. Man's chief concern is to care for his soul. The destiny of souls vary, but the following are common elements in Platonic thought: judgment after death, intermediate state of rewards, purificatory punishment and return of souls to earth in human or animal form. The soul becomes eternal by partaking of eternal truths (ideas).

Mohammedan eschatology has been described as gross, crude, and vivid. Heaven and hell are material and the attainment of either of these states or places is preceded by resurrection and judgment. All non-Moslems are destined to hell which has seven regions. There is an elaborate angelology and the afterlife reflects the high moral and ethical content of the present life which includes prayer, pilgrimage, alms giving, and fasting.

Like other religions, Judaism shows the development of a progressive belief in life after death, from non-existence to Sheol, communion with God, and then resurrection. Sheol is a negative replica of the earthly existence where function rather than form or location is stressed. Most Old Testament passages do not speak of a moral order in Sheol and the distinctive mark of dwellers in Sheol is weakness. This idea helps to explain the condemnation of necromancy since the dead as a whole never had superior knowledge. Thus, communication with the dead was considered a form of idolatry.

In Christianity, life after death is a central concern because of the resurrection of Jesus and his promises to his followers that they shall live on through faith in him. Although there are variations in Jesus' teachings about life beyond this, he does consistently speak of the fact that we reap what we sow, that there is some continuity of identity, an integrity of self that goes beyond the grave, and that he is the means by which one continues to live on. Jesus was concerned with the future life primarily as it had meaning for one's life now.

The philosophers also have had something to say about survival and immortality. The following represent major philosophical "proofs" for the on-going life.

1. Universality of belief. The fact that most people and cultures believe in life after death constitutes a strong case for survival.

2. Pragmatic. Belief in future life promotes public morals and responsibility, makes hope real and puts a brake on opportunistic living in which exploitation often occurs.

3. Teleological. Life ever moves toward fulfillment of purpose. Since perfection is not fully attained in this life, it must have another life to do this. Man's incompleteness "here" points to a completion "there."

4. Analogical. Just as nature dies and lives again (the analogy of metamorphosis), so do humans who are a part of nature.

5. Moral. The aim of life is the furthering of holiness by conformity to moral law. This aim becomes the postulate of infinite progress — well beyond the grave.

6. Righteousness and Justice. Virtue must be rewarded and sin punished. Since both are imperfectly realized here, another sphere of life is required.

7. Ontological. Spirit, from which the soul derives, is eternal. Therefore, the soul, made in the image of Creator Spirit, never dies.

8. Religious. The witness of the Scriptures and faith of major religions attest to the reality of immortality.

9. Phenomenological. Resurrection accounts plus the array of psychical phenomena point to continuance of life beyond death.

One of the more dramatic areas of exploration of life after death is that of psychical research. Researchers are giving special attention to the out-of-body experience (OBE) which is a relatively common experience and one that can be tested and monitored reasonably well. If there is a non-material component of man, which, during life, can leave the body and maintain itself for periods in an exteriorized state or location while exercising hearing, seeing, memory, awareness, and thought processes — then, theoretically, that non-material component may be able to survive death.

There are numerous types of subjective OBE's.

1. Traumatic separation.
   a. Anticipating an accident
   b. In an accident
   c. In childbirth
   d. During surgery, intense pain, coma, under anesthesia
   e. Result of shock

2. Voluntary separation.

3. Dreamtime separation (especially in "lucid" dreams where you are aware of your dreaming).

4. Near-death or severe illness separation.

5. Clinical death separation.

6. Spirit-induced separation.

7. During hypnotic or psychic trance.

8. Bilocation, when unaware of the extended existence.

9. Bilocation, when aware of activity in both existences.

10. An observed OBE double.

11. OBE doubles in the seance room.

12. Piggy-back OBE, where the traveler is unaware that he is a "tour conductor."

13. The "fully operational" OBE, which is seen, touched, converses, eats, drinks, moves objects, writes.

14. At the moment of death.

15. The "Doppelganger" or "reverse OBE" (where consciousness stays in the body but recognizes its double "out there").

The more objective OBE's include:

1. Auditory response, which includes involuntary and voluntary types, where the traveler "hears" something specific, unique, and verifiable while at the remote location.

2. Pre-planned "perspective" cases in which an optical image device in another room is used whereby the target image is purposely distorted at a viewing lens. The subject "travels," views the target through the lens and also without the lens, and reports the two different images.

3. Pre-planned "fly-in" cases where travelers are able to correctly identify staged items at remote locations.

4. Observed apparitions of the living which are verified at both ends by witnesses.

Other evidences for spirit survival of bodily death include the following:

1. Drop-in Communicator. This involves the appearance of an entity where there is no recognition or relationship between the entity and the medium or any of the sitters. The entity is not invited to communicate.

2. Apparitions of the Recent Dead. These have appeared throughout history and numerous cases are recorded in the annals of psychical research.

3. Audible Voice. Subject hears the deceased person's voice.

4. Reports from the Recent Dead. The deceased communicates in some way with the living, sometimes offering important information.

5. Cross Correspondence. A complex mediumistic approach in which fragmentary utterances from different mediums, which have no point or meaning in themselves, but which when pieced together, give a coherent message.

6. Claimed Memories of Former Incarnations. Reincarnation is based on the belief in survival of physical death.

7. Possession. Throughout history, possession by spirits of the deceased has been claimed, although not proven.

8. Survival Codes. Persons develop a code for use in writing an encoded message to be communicated by the writer after his death. A variation of this is some special action each agrees on which is to be effected after one dies.

9. Automatic Writing. Subject writes messages automatically with information from "someone" on the other side.

10. Spirit-recorded Voices. This is the electronic voice phenomenon in which voices of the deceased are heard and recorded on tape.

11. Spirit Photography. Pictures of deceased appear on normal film usually alongside of the images of the live person who is photographed.

12. Materialization. This is the appearance of the deceased in some ectoplasmic form.

13. Handwriting Verification. An apparition produces writing that a graphoanalyst can verify against pre-death writing samples.

14. Photomultiplier Potential. Living tissue emits light, usually ultraviolet, but sometimes visible. When some organisms are damaged or destroyed, light emission increases, possibly indicating new life energies.

15. Experiments at the Moment of Death.
    a. Photography. Photographing corpses at intervals to see the emergence and development of mist-like form. Psychics often claim to see this.
    b. Weight Loss at Moment of Death. Slight weight loss might suggest the departure of some aspect of self.

16. Deathbed Visions. There are many reports of the dying person experiencing the presence of loved ones who predeceased him, religious figures, scenes, and sounds from another world.

17. Apparitions at Moment of Death. At the very moment of death, person experiences the presence of someone who has died or someone who is still living, but not physically present with the dying person at the last moment.

18. Musical Moments. Beautiful music is sometimes heard and keys on instruments are seen to move without anyone being visible. Deathbed music also is often heard by dying persons.

19. Clinical death experiences provide some of the more popular views of life after death. Reports from persons who pass into a temporary state of clinical death marked by absence of heartbeat, respiration, and other vital signs reveal similar experiences regardless of race, culture, background, religion, or social standing. Common elements in these experiences include:

a. Ineffability, in which the experience is beyond description.

b. Noise (buzzing, vibrating, whining) and movement (drifting, floating) through a tunnel, funnel, well, cave, or cylinder, usually with a light at the end.

c. Finding oneself outside the physical body (OBE).

d. Meeting predeceased friends and relatives or spiritual guides who often inform the person he must return to life.

e. Panoramic review of life events, not in a linear, temporal sequence, but actions, thoughts, and consequence happen simultaneously.

f. Not afraid to go through the experience again.

g. Immersion in light with a feeling of warmth, love, and acceptance.

h. Encountering a "presence," a "being of light" who is loving and challenging with such questions as, "What are you doing with your life?"

i. Feelings of ease, peace, well-being and not wanting to return. Hardly any reports of "hell-like" experiences.

j. Experiencing transcendent realms of indescribable beauty and music.

k. Gaining insights about what is on the other side of death.

l. Acquiring positive attitudes toward life; not being afraid to die and a new focus on what is here rather than fearing death.

It must be noted that these glowing reports that come from the other side can be dangerous.

> One nurse on a psychiatric unit reported a patient, who had heard a revived clinical death patient testify to the beauty of the other side, managed to take an overdose. Another nurse, working in a prison infirmary, told of a prisoner who had seen a similar testimony on TV and committed suicide immediately thereafter. A third nurse, working in a nursing home, helped to revive a patient who had clinically died. When he revived, he was very angry with her for two weeks because she had brought him back from his beautiful new life.

> Also there are reports about some unpleasant experiences. One nurse, working with clinical death suicide cases, stated that most of these persons reported feelings of fear, darkness, alienation — feelings that are usually associated with hell rather than heaven.

What meaning do these theological, philosophical, and psychical concepts, theories, beliefs, and experiences concerning life after death have for the living and the dying?

A vital faith in the on-going life affirms that the world of your present consciousness is just one of several or many worlds of consciousness. This can be an exciting awareness, for it can lift you out of your little ghetto of time and place to transcendental dimensions far beyond. A person, to be a person, needs something or someone beyond himself for which to strive. Recognizing other worlds of being can give you new hope in times of despair and provide new horizons when your view of life is dim and limited. Also, if you have faith that there is something in your present life that will outlive it, you can find greater purpose, exhibit more responsibility, find greater joy and peace in life here and now.

Faith in life after death attests to the primacy of the spiritual over the material. In a world where materialism often is rampant, where the god of flesh seems to reign supreme and life becomes so horizontal, faith in the continuance of life promotes the value and validity of life in the spirit and expresses the significance of the vertical dimension in your life on earth. Faith in the primacy of spirit is helpful in dealing with violent and sudden death.

Faith in life after death affirms the sacredness of life and the kinship of life, factors which can be significant for your attitude toward your fellowman as well as toward yourself.

Investigation into the nature of the spirit life by scientists and theologians provides new insights and avenues in your approach to truth. The relation of spirit (energy) to matter is an area under serious study by scientists, and information from those who have experienced communication from the other side can be helpful in advancing this frontier of truth.

Finally, an active faith in life after death can be a welcome boost for the church. The church visible needs the church invisible if the church is to be indivisible. The serious involvement of church leaders and members in the life of the spirit here and in the hereafter can help sharpen the focus of the nature and purpose of the church and bring new power to bear upon the problems that are plaguing both the church and the world.

*Trust in God (and in the being which is maintained by him) does not, then, do away with death: but it makes death such that it opens the way to greater fullness of life. . . . The greater the faith with which one allows death to carry one off, the more will death introduce one to some individually heightened form of existence.*

Pierre Teilhard de Chardin

*I am the resurrection, and the life: he that believeth in me, though he were dead, yet shall he live:*

*And whosoever liveth and believeth in me shall never die.*

Jesus the Christ

*There is a land of the living and a land of the dead and the bridge is love.*

Thornton Wilder

*We are apt to feel as if nothing we could do on earth bears a relation to what the good are doing in a higher world; but it is not so. Heaven and earth are not so far apart. Every disinterested act, every sacrifice to duty, every exertion for the good of "one of the least of Christ's brethren," every new insight into God's works, every new impulse given to the love of truth and goodness, associates us with the departed, brings us nearer to them, and is as truly heavenly as if we were acting, not on earth, but in heaven. The spiritual tie between us and the departed is not felt as it should be. Our union with them daily grows stronger, if we daily make progress in what they are growing in.*

William E. Channing

# Chapter 18

# In Green Pastures and Beside Still Waters

# Meditations for Comfort and Hope

The mystery of death means that there are countless ways to conceive of and experience death and dying. Also, there are many ways to find and to offer comfort and hope for the dying. A passage of scripture, a touch of the hand, a warm embrace, an understanding smile, a sincere dialogue, a poem, beautiful music — any of these and many others can be the key to helping the dying and their loved ones in their journey through the valley of the shadow.

The selections in this chapter are offered as paths along the final journey of the pilgrim on this plane and planet. The pathways are those of the heart.

# I

We are compassed about by a cloud of witnesses, whose hearts throb in sympathy with every effort and struggle, and who thrill with joy at every success. How should this thought check and rebuke every worldly feeling and unworthy purpose, and enshrine us in the midst of a forgetful and unspiritual world, with an atmosphere of heavenly peace! They have overcome — have risen — are around, glorified; but still they remain to us, our assistants, our comforters, and in every hour of darkness their voice speaks to us: "So we grieved, so we struggled, so we fainted, so we doubted; but we have overcome, we have obtained, we have seen, we have found — and in our victory behold the certainty of thy own."

*Harriet Beecher Stowe*

## II

On the day when death will knock at thy door
What wilt thou offer him?
Oh, I will set before my guest the full vessel of my
   life.
I will never let him go with empty hands. . . .
A summons has come and I am ready for my
   journey.

*Rabindranath Tagore*

## III

### Cradled

The door to the future is seldom open,
We know not what lies ahead;
The secret of time's womb is not broken,
Uncertain is one's tread.

But uncertainty, mystery, obscurity,
In the flux of the sifting sands
Have no fearful grip on me
When I know
In life's flow
Every phase
Of my days
Is cradled in God's hands.

*Louis Richard Batzler*

## IV

### A Will and a Way

When God calls me to move beyond this life, I do not wish my vessels to be emptied of the fluid that pulsated and flowed through my body and gave life to it.

Nor do I want to be placed in a concrete vault for protection from the elements that nurtured my body, enlightened my mind and enriched my soul while I walked this planet.

My desire is to rest in a simple pine box beneath the sod which God breathed upon to give me life. And for the marker I ask only for a little tree to be planted which I can nourish and which can be the host for those who would visit this place — a host that can offer shade for my friends and a play place for little children, a sheltering home for the birds and food for the squirrels; a host that will blossom and be a trysting place for lovers and an inspiration to the poet.

Then all who come will see that even death is but a phase of life and an opportunity for love and service to God and His creation.

*Louis Richard Batzler*

## V

Death surrenders us totally to God; it makes us enter into him; we must, in return, surrender ourselves to death with absolute love and self-abandonment — since, when death comes, all we can do is to surrender ourselves completely to the domination and guidance of God. . . . Death has been treated too much as a subject for melancholy reflection, or as an occasion for self-discipline, or as a rather hazy theological entity. . . . What we have to do is to see it in its true context, see it as an active reality, as one more phase, in a world and a "becoming" that are those of our own experience.

*Pierre Teilhard de Chardin*

# VI

## Healing Memories

Too often our remembering is mourning for the dead, literally or figuratively placing wreaths at the grave's head, fretting and regretting. As such, memories become debilitating and disintegrating.

Memories can be vehicles of healing, joy and hope if we can direct them rightly. Let your memories of those loved ones who have passed on be a celebrating of life rather than a centering on death, promoting of love rather than placing lilies, a garnering of gratitude rather than a gathering of grief.

What do we do when we remember those who have passed over?

First, we bring the past immediately into our present and make the fact of those past lives a present reality. In memory, we transcend time and space and make historical facts existential moments. We witness to the unbroken chain of life — to the continuity, the on-goingness of the life of the spirit. Just as every Christian acknowledges that Christ is his contemporary, so do we acknowledge that the lives we remember are contemporaneous with our lives.

In addition to professing the continuity of life, our act of remembrance proclaims the kinship of life. The memory of our loved ones reminds us of that fellowship and spiritual kinship that all humans share and enables us to better understand and relate to our fellowmen here and now.

Remembering is also an expression of gratitude — gratitude for life — for those lives we recall and for our own lives. To regard memory as an act of gratitude is to enrich and enlarge the lives of those who are remembered and those who are remembering. For gratitude is giving, and to give is to live. He who lives in an attitude of gratitude knows that latitude of joy and freedom that has no bounds.

Through our memory of others we can often find new courage, hope and strength for ourselves now and in the days to come. Memory can be a catalyst for commitment, a decision for dedication, a renewal of right relationships with God and our fellowmen.

Memory is an act of love — a love that does not fail, falter or forget; a love that creates new life and continues old life; a love that practices the presence of all of life; a love that bridges the canyons of time and space; a love that binds the wound of severed spirits and frees the minds that are still imprisoned in the caskets of grief.

Thus, memories can be healing if the meaning of memory

   . . . celebrates life rather than calculates death,

   . . . utilizes the power of the past for problems of the present and puts in proper perspective the priorities of the present,

   . . . expresses gratitude for life and gain rather than laments strife and pain,

   . . . centers life around God rather than focuses on sod,

   . . . kindles our love rather than spindles threads of bitterness and weaves a web of woe.

To rightly remember is to dismember death and to reaffirm and renew life.

*Louis Richard Batzler*

# VII

Know that your life is holy and sacred. Know that God gives you hope in your despair, strength in your weakness, joy in your sorrow, comfort in your pain.

Because your life is sacred, your life is precious and your life will be renewed — renewed beyond your greatest imagination. You are thankful now and you rest in the faithfulness and love of God, knowing that in His love He always works for your good.

*Louis Richard Batzler*

# VIII

The senior course of study now was opened up and Jesus entered and became a pupil of the heirophant. He learned the secrets of the mystic lore of Egypt land; the mysteries of life and death and of the worlds beyond the circle of the sun. When he had finished all the studies of the senior course, he went into the Chamber of the Dead, that he might learn the ancient methods of preserving from decay the bodies of the dead; and here he wrought.

And carriers brought the body of a widow's only son to be embalmed; the weeping mother followed close; her grief was great. And Jesus said, Good woman, dry your tears; you follow but an empty house; your son is in it not. You weep because your son is dead. Death is a cruel word; your son can never die. He had a task assigned to do in garb of flesh; he came; he did his work, and then he laid the flesh aside; he did not need it more. Beyond your human sight he has another work to do, and he will do it well, and then pass on to other tasks, and, by and by, he will attain the crown of perfect life.

And what your son has done, and what he yet must do, we all must do. Now if you harbour grief, and give your sorrows vent they will grow greater every day. They will absorb your very life until at last you will be naught but grief, wet down with bitter tears. Instead of helping him you grieve your son by your deep grief. He seeks your solace now as he has ever done; is glad when you are glad; is saddened when you grieve. Go bury deep your woes, and smile at grief, and lose yourself in helping others dry their tears.

With duty done comes happiness and joy; and gladness cheers the hearts of those who have passed on. The weeping woman turned, and went her way to find a happiness in helpfulness; to bury deep her sorrows in a ministry of joy.

Then other carriers came and brought the body of a mother to the Chamber of the Dead; and just one mourner followed; she a girl of tender years. And as the cortege neared the door, the child observed a wounded bird in sore distress; a cruel hunter's dart had pierced its breast. And she left following the dead, and went to help the living bird.

With tenderness and love she folded to her breast the wounded bird, then hurried to her place. And Jesus said to her, Why did you leave your dead to save a wounded bird? The maiden said, This lifeless body needs no help from me; but I can help while yet life is; my mother taught me this. My mother taught that grief and selfish love, and hopes and fears are but reflexes from the lower self; that what we sense are but small waves upon the rolling billows of a life.

These all will pass away; they are unreal. Tears flow from hearts of flesh; the spirit never weeps; and I am longing for the day when I will walk in light, where tears are wiped away. My mother taught that all emotions are the sprays that rise from human loves, and hopes, and fears; that perfect bliss cannot be ours till we have conquered these. And in the presence of that child did Jesus bow his head in reverence. He said, for days and months and years I've sought to learn this highest truth that man can learn on earth, and here a child, fresh brought to earth, has told it all in one short breath.

No wonder David said, O Lord, how excellent is thy name in all the earth! Out of the mouths of babes and sucklings hast thou ordained strength. And then he laid his hand upon the maiden's head, and said, I'm sure the blessings of my Father-God will rest upon you, child, for evermore.

*The Aquarian Gospel of Jesus the Christ*

# IX

Life has meaning, life has plan and purpose;
Man was not created but to perish.
God has fashioned him in His own image,
But a little lower than the angels.
With creations of his mind, man spans the waters,
Fathoms depths and tunnels towering mountains.
Man is master over all creation,
Earth and air, yea, time and space he conquers.
Man's achievements make his life immortal
Though his span of years on earth be ended.
Love and faith and righteous, steadfast striving
Leave their imprints in the hearts of loved ones.
Brick and stone and steel that gird our structures,
All must crumble, in their time be shattered.
Naught remains of all our pride and vaunting,
Save our blessed deeds that are eternal.
When the memories of our dear departed
Spur us onto nobler aspiration,
In our hearts they live enshrined forever,
Though removed from earthly habitation.
When hypocrisy and hate we banish,
When our efforts loose the bonds of evil,
When we feed the hungry, clothe the naked,
Strive for peace, for righteousness and justice —
Yea, 'tis then that we become immortal,
Deathless, timeless, living on in others.

*High Holiday Prayer Book*

## X

My life is but a weaving between God and me,
I do not choose the colors, He worketh steadily.
Oft times He weaveth sorrow, and I in foolish pride,
Forget He sees the upper, and I the underside.
Not till the loom is silent, and shuttles cease to fly,
Will God unroll the canvas and explain the reason
  why.
The dark threads are as needful in the skillful
  Weaver's hand,
As the threads of gold and silver in the pattern He
  has planned.

*Anonymous*

# XI

## A Child is Loaned

"I'll lend you for a little time
  a child of Mine," He said,
"For you to love the while she lives
  and mourn for when she's dead.
It may be six or seven years,
  or twenty-two or three,
But will you, till I call her back,
  take care of her for Me?

She'll bring her charms to gladden you;
  and should her stay be brief,
You'll have her lovely memories
  as solace for your grief.
I cannot promise she will stay,
  since all from earth return,
But there are lessons taught down there
  I want this child to learn.

I've looked this wide world over
  in My search for teachers true,
And from the throngs that crowd life's lanes,
  I have selected you.
Now will you give her all your love,
  nor think the labor vain,
Nor hate Me when I come to call
  and take her back again?"

I fancied that I heard them say:
  "Dear Lord, your will be done.
For all the joy your child shall bring
  the risk of grief we'll run;
We'll shelter her with tenderness,
  we'll love her while we may;

And for the happiness we've known,
   forever grateful stay.

But should the angels call for her
   much sooner than we've planned,
We'll brave the bitter grief that comes
   and try to understand."

*Anonymous*

## XII

Let us, then, learn that we can never be lonely or forsaken in this life. Shall they forget us because they are "made perfect?" Shall they love us the less because they now have power to love us more? If we forget them not, shall they not remember us with God?

No trial, then, can isolate us, no sorrow can cut us off from the Communion of Saints. Kneel down and you are with them; lift up your eyes, and the heavenly world, high above all perturbation, hangs serenely overhead; only a thin veil, it may be, floats between. All whom we loved, and all who loved us, whom we still love no less, while they love us yet more, are ever near, because [they are] ever in His presence in whom we live and dwell.

*Henry Edward Manning*

# XIII

## SEE ME!

What do you see, nurses, what do you see?
Are you thinking when you look at me —
A crabbit old woman, not very wise
Uncertain of habit with faraway eyes
Who dribbles her food and makes no reply
When you say in a loud voice — "I do wish you'd
 try."
Who seems not to notice the things that you do and
 forever is losing a stocking or shoe.
Who, unresisting or not, lets you do as you will
With bathing and feeding, the long day to fill?

Is that what you're thinking, is that what you see?
Then open your eye, nurse, you're not looking at
 me.
I'll tell you who I am as I sit here so still
As I move at your bidding, as I eat at your will.

I'm a small child of ten with a father and mother
Brothers and sisters who love one another.
A young girl of sixteen with wings on her feet
Dreaming that soon a lover she'll meet.

A bride soon at twenty — my heart gives a leap
Remembering the vows that I promised to keep.
At twenty-five now I have young of my own
Who need me to build a secure, happy home.

A woman of thirty, my young now grow fast
Bound together with ties that should last.
At forty my young sons have grown and gone
But my man's beside me to see I don't mourn.
At fifty once more babies play round my knee
Again we know children, my loved ones and me.

Dark days are upon me, my husband is dead.
I look at the future, I shudder with dread.
For my young are all rearing young of their own
And I think of the years and the love that I've
  known.
I'm an old woman now and nature is cruel.
'Tis her jest to make old age look like a fool.
The body, it crumbles, grace and vigour depart
There is a stone where I once had a heart.

But inside this old carcass a young girl still dwells
And now and again my battered heart swells.
I remember the joys, I remember the pain
And I'm loving and living life over again.
I think of the years, all too few, all gone too fast
And accept the stark fact that nothing can last.
So open your eyes, nurses, open and see
Not a crabbit old woman, look closer — SEE ME!

*This poem was found in the belongings of an aged patient who died in a nursing home.*

## XIV

Our fundamental task as living human beings is to struggle against death. But when death comes to us, our faith in life must cause us to give ourselves to death as to a moving toward a greater, more glorious life. To love life and to trust life and the Life Giver so completely that when we approach death we can be thankful for death as well as for life — this is the consciousness that can give us comfort, peace and hope.

To love lavishly what is greater than oneself, to become one with a greater power always involves a kind of death of the self. Death is bearable, is acceptable and even beautiful when one sees it as a passage toward union with God in a new and more glorious way — a majestic and meaningful metamorphosis and a transcendence beyond our greatest expectations.

*Louis Richard Batzler*

## XV

### God Is Here and Now

God is your refuge and strength.
God's love for you is forever.
God's light surrounds you, permeates
   and dispels your darkness.

God's power gives you strength now
   in your weakness.
God's pardon cleanses you.
God's promises give you hope.

God's presence is always with you
   in pain and pleasure, sickness
   and health,
Sorrow and joy, failure and success,
   in death and life.
God's protection saves you from all
   harm, from all evil.

God's wisdom directs and leads you.
God's peace calms you.

God's purpose is that your life —
   precious, sacred and made in His
   image — will continue in a new and
   more glorious way.

So love, thank and praise God
   now and always.

*Louis Richard Batzler*

# XVI

After having perceived you as he is "a greater than myself," grant *when my hour comes*, that I may recognize you under the species of each alien or hostile force that seems bent upon destroying or uprooting me. When the signs of age begin to mark my body (and still more when they touch my mind); when the ill that is to diminish me or carry me off strikes from without or is born within me; when the painful moment comes in which I suddenly awaken to the fact that I am ill or growing old; and above all at that last moment when I feel I am losing hold of myself and am absolutely passive within the hands of the great unknown forces that have formed me; in all those dark moments, O God, grant that I may understand that it is you (provided only my faith is strong enough) who are painfully parting the fibres of my being in order to penetrate to the very marrow of my substance and bear me away within yourself. . . .

Teach me *to treat my death as an act of communion.*
*Pierre Teilhard de Chardin*

# XVII

## Of Meditation on Death

Very quickly there will be an end of thee here; see therefore to thy state. Today man is; tomorrow he is gone. And when he is out of sight, quickly is he out of mind. Oh, the stupidity and hardness of man's heart, which thinketh only upon the present and doth not rather regard what is to come! Thou oughtest so to order thyself in all thy thoughts and actions as if today thou wert to die. If thou hadst a good conscience, thou wouldst not greatly fear death. It were better to avoid sin than to escape death. If today thou art not prepared, how wilt thou be so tomorrow! Tomorrow is uncertain, and how knowest thou that thou shalt live till tomorrow!

What availeth it to live long when there is so small amendment in us? Alas, length of days doth not always better us, but often rather increaseth our sins. Oh, that we had spent but one day in this world thoroughly well! Many there are who reckon years of conversion; and yet full slender often times is the fruit of amendment. If to die be accounted dreadful, to live long may perhaps prove more dangerous. Happy is he that always hath the hour of his death before his eyes, and daily prepareth himself to die. If at any time thou hast seen a man die, reflect that thou must also pass the same way.

When it is morning, think that thou mayest die before night; and when evening cometh, dare not to promise thyself the next morning. Be thou therefore always in readiness, and so lead thy life that death may never take thee unprepared. Many die suddenly and when they look not for it, for the Son of

Man will come in an hour when we think not. When that last hour shall come, thou wilt begin to have a far different opinion of thy whole life that is past, and be exceeding sorry that thou hast been so careless and remiss.

Oh, how wise and happy is he that now laboreth to be such a one in his life as he will desire to be found at the hour of death! A perfect contempt of the world, a fervent desire to go forward in all virtue, a love of discipline, a laborious repentance, a ready obedience, a denying of ourselves and an endurance of any affliction whatsoever for the love of Christ, will give us great confidence that we shall die happily. Whilst thou art in health thou mayest do much good, but when thou art sick, I see not what thou wilt be able to do. Few are improved by sickness; so also they who wander much abroad, seldom become holy.

Trust not to friends and kindred, neither do thou put off the care of thy soul's welfare till hereafter; for man will forget thee sooner than thou art aware of. It is better to look to it betime and to send some good before thee, than to trust to the help of others after thy death. If thou be not careful for thyself now, who will be careful for thee hereafter? Time now is very precious: now is the acceptable time; now is the day of salvation. But alas! that thou shouldst spend time so idly here in which thou mightest purchase life eternal. The time will come when thou shalt desire one day or hour to amend in, and I know not that it will be granted thee.

O beloved, from how great danger mightest thou deliver thyself, from how great fear free thyself, if thou wouldst be ever fearful and mindful of death!

Labor now so to live, that at the hour of death thou mayest rather rejoice than fear. Learn now to die to the world, that thou mayest then begin to live with Christ. Learn how to contemn all things, that thou mayest then freely go to Christ. Chastise thy body now by penance that thou mayest then have assured confidence.

Ah, fool! Why dost thou think to live long, when thou canst not promise to thyself one day? How many have been deceived and suddenly snatched away! How often dost thou hear these reports: Such a man is slain, another man is drowned, a third has broken his neck with a fall from some high place; this man died eating, and that man playing! One perished by fire, another by the sword, another of the plague, another by the hands of robbers. Thus death is the end of all, and man's life suddenly passeth away like a shadow.

Who shall remember thee when thou art dead, and who shall pray for thee? Do now, even now, my beloved, whatsoever thou art able to do; for thou knowest not when thou shalt die nor what shall befall thee after thy death. Now, whilst thou hast time, heap unto thyself everlasting riches. Think on nothing but the salvation of thy soul, care for nothing but the things of God. Make now friends to thyself by knowing the saints of God, and imitating their actions, that when thou failest, they may receive thee into everlasting dwellings.

Keep thyself as a stranger and pilgrim upon the earth, who hath nothing to do with the affairs of this world. Keep thy heart free and lifted up to God, because thou hast here no lasting city. Send thither thy daily prayers and sighs together with thy tears, that after death thy spirit may be found worthy to pass in felicity to the Lord. Amen.

*Thomas á Kempis*

*The Reality of Life is Life itself, whose beginning is not in the womb, and whose ending is not in the grave. For the years that pass are naught but a moment in eternal life; and the world of matter and all in it but a dream compared to the awakening which we call the terror of Death.*

Kahlil Gibran

*In the shadow of death, let us not look back to the past, but look forward, even in the totality of darkness, to the dawn of God's love and mercy.*

Louis Richard Batzler

# Chapter 19

# Organizational Resources on Death and Dying

The avoidance and ambivalence that most Americans manifest concerning the subject of death and death-related topics is indicated not only by their confusion in dealing with the dying and their own death, but also by their ignorance concerning the funeral, burial, financial and legal matters associated with death. We adequately prepare ourselves for so many events in life, but for the great event of death, most prepare very little.

This confusion and inadequacy is not due to a lack of professional persons, materials and organizations that are available to provide information and assistance for virtually every need during illness, at the time of death and after death. The following are reliable and helpful organizational resources.[1] Valuable written resources are included in the bibliography.

Alan Foss Leukemia Memorial Fund
730 E. 79th Street
Brooklyn, NY 11236
  Provides economic and emotional support to leukemia patients and families.
Also sponsors research.

ALSAC (Aiding Leukemia Stricken American
    Children)
St. Jude's Children's Research Hospital
539 Lane Avenue
Memphis, TN 38105
   St. Jude's is a leading national center for the
study and treatment of childhood cancers.

American Association of Suicidology
Department of Psychiatry
Baylor College of Medicine
1200 Moursund
Houston, TX 77030
   The association supports research, educational
programs and publishes.

American Cancer Society, Inc.
777 Third Avenue
New York, NY 10017
   The society has divisional offices in every state
and regional offices in many cities. It has many
printed and audiovisual resources for professionals and the public.

American Heart Association
7320 Greenville Avenue
Dallas, TX 75231
   There are chapters in every state and many local
offices which direct educational programs, conduct research and publish.

Candlelighters Foundation
123 C Street, SE
Washington, DC 20003
   A national federation formed to lobby for federal funding of cancer research and as a support

group mainly for parents with children suffering from or lost to cancer.

Center for Death Education and Research
1167 Social Science Building
University of Minnesota
Minneapolis, MN 55455

Sponsors research on death, dying, grief and bereavement; provides resource material and speakers.

Compassionate Friends
P.O. Box 1347
Oak Brook, IL 60521

A support group with chapters in various cities, for parents who have lost children. Provides literature, information and assistance.

Concern for Dying: An Educational Council
250 W. 57th Street
New York, NY 10107

Main purpose is to protect patient autonomy in regard to treatment during terminal illness. Publishes newsletter, has film library, speakers bureau and holds conferences.

Continental Association of Funeral
   and Memorial Societies
1828 L Street, NW, Suite 1100
Washington, DC 20036

Offers information and assistance in funeral planning and arrangements.

Euthanasia Foundation
250 W. 57th Street
New York, NY 10019

Information and publications on euthanasia.

Forum for Death Education and
Counseling, Inc.
P.O. Box 1226
Arlington, VA 22210
Primarily for professionals, prepares educational materials, workshops. Publishes *Omega*, a scholarly journal.

Foundation of Thanatology
630 West 168th Street
New York, NY 10032
An educational and scientific organization primarily of scholars. Conducts research, publishes and sponsors symposia.

Grief Education Institute
6198 S. Westview
Littleton, CO 80120
Offers grief counseling for all types of clients, conducts programs, publishes newsletter.

The International Association for
Near-Death Studies, Inc.
Box U-20, University of Connecticut
Storrs, CT 06268
Encourages and supports research, sponsors symposia, maintains archives related to near-death experiences.

International Association for Suicide Prevention
University of California Medical Center
San Francisco, CA 94143
Provides an international forum for exchange of research, information and experience on suicide. Also sponsors research and publishes.

Living Bank
P.O. Box 6725
Houston, TX 77005

A nonprofit registry, coordinating and distributing agency and information center for anatomical gifts.

Make Today Count
P.O. Box 303
Burlington, IA 52601

Provides information and assistance for persons with life-threatening illnesses and their families. Also publishes materials for professional caretakers.

Muscular Dystrophy Association
    of America, Inc.
810 Seventh Avenue
New York, NY 10019

Provides medical treatment, orthopedic appliances, sponsors research and publishes.

National Abortion Rights Action League
706 Seventh Street, SE
Washington, DC 20003

A political, social, legal action group which aims to promote safe, legal abortion for all women. Publishes newsletters and periodical.

National Association for Mental Health
1800 North Kent Street
Arlington, VA 22209

Sponsors research, publishes, distributes materials on behalf of the mentally ill. Includes topics on aging, nursing homes, suicide, widowhood and coping with death in families.

National Cancer Foundation, Inc.
One Park Avenue
New York, NY 10016
   Promotes programs and research of professional
and psychosocial services to advanced cancer pa-
tients and their families.

National Council of Senior Citizens
1511 K Street, N.W.
Washington, DC 20005
   An education and action group for the aging.

National Easter Seal Society for
      Crippled Children and Adults
2023 West Ogden Avenue
Chicago, IL 60612
   Works primarily on behalf of the physically
handicapped.

National Foundation — March of Dimes
Box 2000
White Plains, NY 10602
   Main aim is to protect the unborn and new-
born. Promotes research, publishes educational
material.

National Funeral Directors Association
135 West Wells Street
Milwaukee, WI 53203
   Provides information and assistance for funeral
and burial matters.

National Hospice Organization
1311A Dolley Madison Boulevard
McLean, VA 22101
   Coordinates hospice work, recommends stan-

dards, publishes training materials, monitors legislation.

National Kidney Foundation
116 East 27th Street
New York, NY 10016
   Sponsors research, fosters improved patient services, educates.

National Multiple Sclerosis Society
257 Park Avenue South
New York, NY 10010
   Serves patients, provides counseling, publishes and sponsors research.

National Research and Information Center
National Foundation of Funeral Service
1600 Central Street
Evanston, IL 60201
   Encourages and facilitates research into death-related issues in a variety of scholarly fields.

National Right to Life Committee
Suite 341
National Press Building
529 14th Street, N.W.
Washington, DC 20045
   Provides information and assistance in anti-abortion, anti-euthanasia concerns.

National Sudden Infant Death
     Syndrome Foundation
310 South Michigan Avenue
Chicago, IL 60604
   Assists parents, educates, promotes research and publishes.

Parents of Murdered Children
1739 Bella Vista
Cincinnati, OH 45237

Offers help to families cruelly bereaved. Provides on-going emotional support for parents by phone, mail, in person, group meetings and through literature.

Psychical Research Foundation, Inc.
Duke Station
Durham, NC 27706

Researches and publishes material on life after death.

St. Francis Burial and Counseling Society, Inc.
1768 Church Street, N.W.
Washington, DC 20036

Publishes, provides information and counseling on death and dying.

Shanti Nilaya
26210 Lake Wohlford Road
Valley Center, CA 92082

Center for healing and investigation of death.

SHANTI Project
1137 Colusa Avenue
Berkeley, CA 94707

Offers counseling services for bereaved, provides training, conducts research.

Stroke Club of America
805 12th Street
Galveston, TX 77550

Helps stroke victims and families, educates and publishes.

THEOS Foundation
11609 Frankstown Road
Pittsburgh, PA 15235

Nonsectarian Christian ministry to the widowed.

Widow to Widow Program
58 Fernwood Road
Boston, MA 02115

A support group for widows.

# Reference Notes

Chapter 1

1. In 1978 an extensive mail survey of four-year colleges and universities with 63.6 percent response revealed that 1,000 death courses were offered which enrolled about 30,000 students.

   Cumming, V.A. *On Death Education in Colleges and Universities in the United States,* 1977. A paper read at the conference of the Forum for Death Education & Counseling. Washington, D.C., September, 1978.

2. A survey of 113 medical schools in 1975 showed that 7 had a full-term course on death; 44 had a "minicourse" and 42 a lecture or two. Only 71 percent of the schools require that at least half of their students be *exposed* to any death education.

   Dickinson, G.E. "Death Education in U.S. Medical Schools." *Journal of Medical Education,* 1976, 51(2), 134-136.

   Also see Bugen, L.A. "Death Education: Perspectives for Schools and Communities" in L.A. Bugen (ed.) *Death and Dying: Theory, Research, Practice.* Dubuque, IA: Brown, 1979, 237-249.

3. Leviton, D. "The Scope of Death Education."
*Death Education*, 1977 1(1), 41-55.

Pine, V.R. "A Socio-historical Portrait of Death
Education." *Death Education*, 1977, 1(1), 57-84.

Chapter 2

1. An interesting phenomenon that is emerging
   concerning preoccupation with death is the increasing use of the death theme in advertising.
   Beer, cancer, and insurance advertisements are
   including the death theme to sell products and
   ideas. Because death is universal, exciting, fearful, and mysterious — all of which are attrac-
   tive, it is understandable why death is used as a
   sales pitch and probably will become more
   prevalent in the future.

2. Schneidman, E.S. "The College Student and
   Death" in Feifel, H. (ed.) *New Meanings of
   Death*. N.Y.: McGraw-Hill, Inc., 1977, 70.

Chapter 3

1. Yalom, I.D. *Existential Psychotherapy*. N.Y.:
   Basic Books, Inc., 1980, 35.

Chapter 4

1. See Pattison, E.M. *The Experience of Dying*. Englewood Cliffs, N.J.: Prentice-Hall, Inc., 1977,
   44-59.

Chapter 5

1. See Wolff, K. "Helping Elderly Patients Face the
   Fear of Death." *Hospital Community Psychiatry*,

1967, 13, 142-144. This study notes that restlessness and insomnia in the elderly are frequently caused by the fear of dying.

## Chapter 6

1. See Choron, J. *Death and Modern Man*. N.Y.: Collier Books, 1964, 112-126.

## Chapter 7

1. Also see Achte, K.A. and Vauhkonen, M.L. "Cancer and the Psyche," *Omega*, 1971, 2, 45-56. The authors conclude that most persons wish to be told of their terminal condition and suffer no permanent negative consequences because of being informed.

2. Montgomery, D.W. *Healing and Wholeness*. Richmond: John Knox Press, 1971, 160-163.

## Chapter 9

1. See Barry, H. "Orphanhood as a Factor in Psychosis." *Journal of Abnormal and Social Psychology*, 1936, 36, 431-438.

   Beck, A., Sathi, B., and Tuthil, R. "Childhood Bereavement and Adult Depression." *Archives of Neurology and Psychiatry*, 1963, 9, 295-302.

2. Baer, R. "The Sick Child Knows." In Standard, S. and Nathan, H. (Eds.) *Should The Patient Know The Truth*. N.Y.: Springer, 1955, 100-106.

3. Spinetta, J.J., Rigler, D., & Karon, M. "Anxiety in The Dying Child." *Pediatrics*, 1973, 52(6), 841-845. In a study of 25 leukemic children aged 6-10, the authors conclude that dying children

may understand that they are going to die before they are able to say so in adult terms.

4. Waechter, E.H. "Children's Awareness of Fatal Illness." *American Journal of Nursing*, 1971, 71(6), 1168-1172.

5. Wiener, J.M. "Response of Medical Personnel to the Fatal Illness of A Child." In Schoenberg, B., Carr, A.C., Peretz, D., and Kutscher, A.H. (Eds.) *Loss and Grief: Psychological Management in Medical Practice*, N.Y.: Columbia U. Press, 1970, 102-115. Also see Wiener, J.M. "Reaction of the Family to the Fatal Illness of A Child." *ibid.*, 87-101.

6. See Bluebond — Langner, M. "Meanings of Death to Children." In Feifel, H. (ed.) *New Meanings of Death*. N.Y.: McGraw-Hill Book Co., 1977, 47-66.

7. See Easson, W.M. *The Dying Child: The Management of the Child or Adolescent Who Is Dying*. Springfield, Ill.: Thomas, 1970.

   Also see Evans, A.E., and Edin, S. "If A Child Must Die." *The New England Journal of Medicine*, 1968, 278(3), 138-142.

Chapter 10

1. Caldwell, D. and Mishara, B.L. "Research On Attitudes of Medical Doctors Toward Dying Patients: A Methodological Problem." *Omega*, 1972, (3), 341-346.

   Also see Schulz, R. and Aderman, D. "How the Medical Staff Copes With Dying Patients: A Critical Review." *Omega*, 1976, 7(1), 11-21.

2. Penzer, M. "An Interview With Ram Dass." *Mandalama Journal*, December, 1981, 3.

3. Rea, M.P., Greenspoon, G. and Spilka, B. "Physicians and The Terminal Patient: Some Selected Attitudes and Behavior." *Omega*, 1975 6(4), 291-302.

4. Oken, D. "What to Tell Cancer Patients: A Study of Medical Attitudes." *Journal of American Medical Association*, 1961, 175, 1120-1128.

5. Achte, K.A. and Vauhkonen, M.L. "Cancer and the Psyche." *Omega*, 1971, (2), 45-56.

6. Bean, W.B. "On Death." *Archives of Internal Medicine*, vol. 101, (June, 1958), 201. Also see above, Chapter 7, No. 3.

7. Laforet, E.G. "The Hopeless Case." *Archives of Internal Medicine*, vol. 112, (September, 1963), 317.

8. Penzer, M. *op. cit.*, 6.

9. Liston, E.H. "Education of Death and Dying: A Survey of American Medical Schools." *Journal of Medical Education*, 1973, 48, 577-578.

10. Dickinson, G.E. "Death Education in U.S. Medical Schools." *Journal of Medical Education*, 1976, 51(2), 134-136.

Chapter 11

1. For more detailed information on bereaved siblings, see Chapter 9 above.

Chapter 15

1. Relaxation tapes and printed materials are avail-

able from the *Gotach Center for Health*, 7051 Poole Jones Rd., Box 606, Frederick, Md. 21701.

2. See Chapter 16 for some examples of Values Clarification and Goal Setting. Also see Simon, S.B., Howe, L.W. and Kirschenbaum, H. *Values Clarification*. N.Y.: Hart Publishing Co., 1972.

3. See Tauraso, N. and Batzler, L.R. *How To Benefit from Stress*, and *Awaken the Genius in Your Child*. Frederick, Md.: Hidden Valley Press, 1979 and 1981.

4. *Ibid*.

5. See Moody, R.A. *Laugh After Laugh*. Jacksonville: Headwaters Press, 1978.

6. Music tapes for the dying and caretakers are available from the *Gotach Center for Health*.

Chapter 19

1. For other organizations, see Wass, H., Corr, C.A., Pacholski, R.A., Sanders, C.M. *Death Education: An Annotated Resource Guide*. Washington: Hemisphere Publ. Corp., 1980, 249-268.

# Bibliography

This bibliography is primarily a working bibliography for reference to basic and relevant sources. It does not include all the works mentioned in the Reference Notes.

Bailis, L.A. "Death In Children's Literature: A Conceptual Analysis," *Omega*, 1977-78, 8(4), 295-303.

Barton, D. *Dying and Death: A Clinical Guide For Caregivers*. Baltimore: Williams and Wilkins, 1977.

Becker, E. *The Denial of Death*. NY: The Free Press, 1973.

Bernstein, J.E. *Books to Help Children Cope With Separation and Loss*, NY: R.R. Bowker, 1977.

Bernstein, J.E. *Loss: And How to Cope With It*. NY: Seabury Press, 1977.

Bowers, M.K., Jackson, E.N., Knight, J.A., and LeShan, L. *Counseling The Dying*. NY: Jason Aronson, 1975.

Brim, O.G., Jr., Freeman, H.E., Levine, S., and Scotch, N.A. (Eds.) *The Dying Patient*. NY: Russell Sage Foundation, 1970.

Browing, M.H., and Lewis, E.P. (Comps.) *The Dying Patient: A Nursing Perspective*. NY: The American Journal of Nursing Co., 1972.

Bugen, L.A. (Ed.) *Death and Dying: Theory/Research/Practice*. Dubuque, IA: Brown, 1979.

Burton, L. (Ed.) *Care of The Child Facing Death*. London: Routledge, Kegan, Paul, 1974.

Caughill, R.E. (Ed.) *The Dying Patient: A Supportive Approach*. Boston: Little, Brown, 1976.

Choron, J. *Death and Western Thought*. NY: Macmillan, 1963.

Croissant, K. and Dees, K. *Continuum: The Immortality Principle*. San Bernardino: Franklin Press, 1978.

Davidson, G.W. *The Hospice: Development and Administration*. Washington, DC: Hemisphere, 1978.

Dahlgren, T., and Prager-Decker, I. "A Unit on Death For Primary Grades." *Health Education*, 1979, 10(1), 36-39.

Easson, W.M. *The Dying Child: The Management of The Child Or Adolescent Who Is Dying*. Springfield, IL: Thomas, 1970.

Earle, A.M., Angondizzo, N.T., and Kutscher, A.H. (Eds.) *The Nurse As Caregiver for The Terminal Patient and His Family*. NY: Columbia U. Press, 1976.

Farberow, N.L., and Shneidman, E.S. (Eds.) *The Cry for Help*. NY: McGraw-Hill, 1961.

Farberow, N.L. *Bibliography on Suicide and Suicide Prevention: 1897-1957, 1958-1967*. (Dept. of Health, Education, and Welfare; Public Health Service, No. 1970). Rockville, MD: NIMH, 1969.

Feifel, H. (Ed.) *The Meaning of Death*. NY: McGraw-Hill, 1959.

Feifel, H. *New Meanings of Death*. NY: McGraw-Hill, 1977.

Friedman, R. and Gradstein, B. *Surviving Pregnancy Loss*. Boston: Little, Brown & Co., 1982.

Fulton, R. (Ed.) in collaboration with R. Bendiksen *Death and Identity*. (Rev. ed.) Bowie, MD: The Charles Press, 1976.

Fulton, R., Carlson, J., Krohn, K., Markusen, E., and Owen, G. *Death, Grief, and Bereavement: A Bibliography, 1845-1975*. NY: Arno Press, 1977.

Garfield, C.A. *Psychosocial Care of the Dying Patient*. NY: McGraw-Hill, 1978.

Garfield, C.A. *Stress and Survival: The Emotional Realities of Life-Threatening Illness*. St. Louis: Mosby, 1979.

Glaser, B. and Strauss, A. *Awareness of Dying*. Chicago: Aldine, 1965.

Gordon, A. and Klass, D. *They Need To Know: How To Teach Children About Death*. Englewood Cliffs, NJ: Prentice-Hall, 1979.

Grollman, E.A. (Ed.) *Explaining Death to Children*. Boston: Beacon, 1967.

Grollman, E.A. (Ed.) *Concerning Death: A Practical Guide For The Living*. Boston: Beacon, 1974.

Grollman, E.A. *Talking About Death*. Boston: Beacon, 1970.

Hart, H. *The Enigma of Survival: The Case For and Against an After Life*. Springfield, IL: Chas. C. Thomas, 1959.

Hick, J. *Death and Eternal Life*. NY: Harper and Row, 1976.

Irion, P.E. *The Funeral and The Mourners*. Nashville: Abingdon, 1954.

Jackson, E.N. *Telling A Child About Death*. NY: Hawthorn Books, Inc., 1965.

Jackson, E.N. *Understanding Grief: Its Roots, Dynamics and Treatment*. Nashville, TN: Abingdon, 1957.

Kastenbaum, R. *Death, Society, and Human Experience*. St. Louis, MO: C. V. Mosby Co., 1977.

Kastenbaum, R. and Aisenberg, R. *The Psychology of Death*. NY: Springer Publishing, 1972.

Kohl, M. (Ed.) *Beneficient Enthanasia*. Buffalo, NY: Prometheus, 1975.

Kubler-Ross, E. *On Death and Dying*. NY: Macmillan, 1969.

Kutscher, A.H. Jr., and Kutscher, A.H. *A Bibliography of Books on Death, Bereavement, Loss and Grief: 1935-1968*. NY: Health Sciences Pub. Corp., 1969.

Langer, M. *Learning to Live As A Widow*. NY: Julian Messner, 1957.

Lewis, C.S. *A Grief Observed*. NY: Seabury Press, 1963.

McGrory, A. *A Well Model Approach To The Dying Client*. NY: McGraw-Hill, 1978.

Miller, A.J. and Acri, M.J. *Death: A Bibliographical Guide*. Metuchen, NJ: Scarecrow, 1977.

Mills, L.O. (Ed.) *Perspectives On Death*. Nashville: Abingdon, 1969.

Mitford, J. *The American Way of Death*. Greenwich, CT: Fawcett Publications, 1963.

Montgomery, D.W. *Healing and Wholeness*. Richmond: John Knox Press, 1971.

Moody, R.A., Jr. *Laugh After Laugh*. Jacksonville: Headwaters Press, 1978.

Moody, R.A., Jr. *Life After Life*. Atlanta: Mockingbird Books, 1975.

Moody, R.A., Jr. *Reflections on Life After Life*. Atlanta: Mockingbird Books, 1977.

Myers, F.W.H. *Human Personality and its Survival of Bodily Death*. NY: University Book, Inc., 1961.

Neale, R.E. *The Art of Dying*. NY: Harper and Row, 1973.

Osis, K. and Haraldsson, E. *At The Hour of Death*. NY: Avon Books, 1979.

Parkes, C.M. *Bereavement: Studies of Grief in Adult Life*. NY: International Universities Press, 1972.

Pattison, E.M. *The Experience of Dying*. Englewood Cliffs, NY: Prentice-Hall, 1977.

Pendleton, E. (Compiler) *Too Old to Cry . . . Too Young To Die*. Nashville: T. Nelson Pub., 1980.

Poteet, G.H. *Death and Dying: A Bibliography (1950-1974)*. Troy, NY: Whitson, 1976.

Prentice, A.E. *Suicide: A Selective Bibliography of More Than 2200 Items*. Metuchen, NJ: Scarecrow, 1974.

Prichard, E.R., Collard, J., Orcutt, B.A., Kutscher, A.H., Seeland, I., and Lefkowitz, N. (Eds.) *Social Work With The Dying Patient and the Family*. NY: Columbia U. Press, 1977.

Prince, A. *Death and Dying: A Mediagraphy. An Annotated Listing of Audiovisual Materials*. Seattle, WA: U. of Washington and Allied Memorial Council, 1977.

Quint, J. *The Nurse and the Dying Patient*. NY: Macmillan, 1967.

Rawlings, M. *Beyond Death's Door*. Nashville: Thos. Nelson Inc. Publishers, 1978.

Rawlings, M. *Before Death Comes*. Nashville: Thos. Nelson Inc. Publishers, 1980.

Ring, K. *Life At Death: A Scientific Investigation of the Near-Death Experience*. NY: Quill, 1982.

Schiff, H.S. *The Bereaved Parent*. NY: Crown, 1977.

Schulz, R. *The Psychology of Death, Dying, and Bereavement*. Reading, MA: Addison-Wesley, 1978.

Schoenberg, B., Carr, A.C., Peretz, D., and Kutscher, A.H. (Eds.) *Loss and Grief: Psychological Management In Medical Practice*. NY: Columbia U., 1970.

Schoenberg, B., Gerber, I., Wiener, A., Kutscher, A.H., Peretz, D., and Carr, A. (Eds.) *Bereavement: Its Psychosocial Aspects*. NY: Columbia U. Press, 1975.

Sell, I. *Dying and Death: An Annotated Bibliography*. NY: Tiresias Press, 1977.

Shapiro, S.I. *Instructional Resources For Teaching the Psychology of Death and Dying*. Honolulu: U. of Hawaii, 1973.

Simon, S.B., Howe, L.W., and Kirschenbaum, H. *Values Clarification*. NY: Hart Publishing Co., 1972.

Standard, S. and Nathan, H. (Eds.) *Should The Patient Know The Truth*. NY: Springer, 1955.

Stoddard, S. *The Hospice Movement: A Better Way of Caring for The Dying*. Briarcliff Manor, NY: Stein and Day, 1978.

Tauraso, N. and Batzler, L.R. *Awaken The Genius in Your Child*. Frederick, MD: Hidden Valley Press, 1981.

Tauraso, N. and Batzler, L.R. *How to Benefit From Stress*. Frederick, MD: Hidden Valley Press, 1979.

Triche, C.W. II, and Triche, D.S. *The Euthanasia Controversy, 1812-1974: A Bibliography With Select Annotations*. Troy, NY: Whitston, 1975.

Wass, H., Corr, C.A., Pacholski, R.A., Sanders, C.M. *Death Education. An Annotated Resource Guide*. Washington, DC: Hemisphere Publ. Corp., 1980.

Wass, H. (Ed.) *Dying: Facing The Facts*. Washington, DC: Hemisphere, 1979.

Weisman, A.D. *On Dying and Denying: A Psychiatric Study of Terminality*. NY: Behavioral Publications, 1972.

White, J. *A Practical Guide to Death and Dying*. Wheaton, IL: The Theosophical Publishing House, 1980.

Wilcox, S.G. and Sutton, M. (Eds.) *Understanding Death and Dying: An Interdisciplinary Approach*. Port Washington, NY: Alfred, 1977.

Yalom, I.D. *Existential Psychotherapy*. NY: Basic Books, Inc., 1980.

# Journals, Periodicals, and Newsletters

American Journal of Nursing.

The Archives of The Foundation of Thanatology.

Archives of Internal Medicine.

Archives of Neurology and Psychiatry.

The Bioethics Digest.

Bulletin of the Continental Association of Funeral and Memorial Societies, Inc.

The Compassionate Friends National Newsletter.

Eclipse: The Shanti Project Newsletter.

Death Education: Pedagogy, Counseling, Care — An International Quarterly.

Essence: Issues in the Study of Aging, Dying, and Death.

Forum for Death Education and Counseling: Newsletter.

Health Education.

Hospital Community Psychiatry.

Journal of Abnormal and Social Psychology.

Journal of American Medical Association.

Journal of Medical Education.

Make Today Count.

Mandalama Journal.

New Advances in Thanatology.

The New England Journal of Medicine.

Newsletter of the National Hospice Organization.

Omega: Journal of Death and Dying.

Pediatrics.

Psychology Today.

St. Francis Burial and Counseling Society Newsletter.

Suicide and Life-Threatening Behavior.

Thanatology Today Newsletter.

Thanatos: A Realistic Journal Concerning Dying, Death, and Bereavement.

Theta: A Journal for Research on the Question of Survival After Death.

# Audiovisual Resources

Audiovisual resources are plentiful. The largest and most complete annotated list of educational audiovisual materials available in the area of death and dying can be found in Wass, H., Corr, C.A., Pacholski, R.A., and Sanders, C.M. *Death Education: An Annotated Resource Guide*. Washington, DC: Hemisphere Publ. Corp., 1980.